Technology

GALLUP
MAJOR TRENDS & EVENTS
The Pulse of Our Nation: 1900 to the Present

Abortion

Drug & Alcohol Abuse

Health Care

Immigration

Marriage & Family Issues

Obesity

Race Relations

Technology

GALLUP
MAJOR TRENDS & EVENTS
The Pulse of Our Nation: 1900 to the Present

Technology

Hal Marcovitz

Produced by OTTN Publishing, Stockton, New Jersey

Mason Crest Publishers
370 Reed Road
Broomall, PA 19008
www.masoncrest.com

First printing

1 3 5 7 9 8 6 4 2

Library of Congress Cataloging-in-Publication Data

Marcovitz, Hal.
    Technology / Hal Marcovitz.
        p. cm. — (Gallup major trends and events)
    Includes bibliographical references and index.
    ISBN-13: 978-1-59084-969-9 (hc)
    ISBN-10: 1-59084-969-8 (hc)
    1. Technology—Social aspects—Juvenile literature.
    2. Technology—History—Juvenile literature. 3. Technology—United
    States—Juvenile literature. I. Title. II. Series.
    T14.5.M367 2006
    303.48'3'0973—dc22
                        2005016297

TABLE OF CONTENTS

Introduction

By Alec Gallup, Chairman, The Gallup Poll

Photo by Eric Olesen

In ways both obvious and subtle, the United States of today differs significantly from the United States that existed at the turn of the 20th century. In 1900, for example, America had not yet taken its place among the world's most influential nations; today the United States stands by itself as the globe's lone superpower. The 1900 census counted about 76 million Americans, largely drawn from white European peoples such as the English, Irish, and Germans; 100 years later the U.S. population was approaching 300 million, and one in every eight residents was of Hispanic origin. In the first years of the 20th century, American society offered women few opportunities to pursue professional careers, and, in fact, women had not yet gained the right to vote. Though slavery had been abolished, black Americans 100 years ago continued to be treated as second-class citizens, particularly in the South, where the Jim Crow laws that would endure for another half-century kept the races separate and unequal.

The physical texture and the pace of American life, too, were much different 100 years ago—or, for that matter, even 50 years ago. Accelerating technological and scientific progress, a hallmark of modern times, has made possible a host of innovations that Americans today take for granted but that would have been unimaginable three generations ago—from brain scans to microwave ovens to cell phones, laptop computers, and the Internet.

No less important than the material, social, and political changes the United States has witnessed over the past century are the changes in American attitudes and perceptions. For example, the way Americans relate to their government and their fellow citizens, how they view marriage and child-rearing norms, where they set the boundary between society's responsibilities and the individual's rights and freedoms—all are key components of Americans' evolving understanding of their nation and its place in the world.

The books in this series examine important issues that have perennially concerned (and sometimes confounded) Americans since the turn of the 20th century. Each volume draws on an array of sources to provide vivid detail and historical context. But, as suggested by the series title, GALLUP MAJOR TRENDS AND EVENTS: THE PULSE OF OUR NATION, 1900 TO THE PRESENT, these books make particular use of the Gallup Organization's vast archive of polling data.

There is perhaps no better source for tracking and understanding American public opinion than Gallup, a name that has been synonymous with opinion polling for seven decades. Over the years, Gallup has elicited responses from more than 3.5 million people on more than 125,000 questions. In 1936 the organization, then known as the American Institute of Public Opinion, emerged into the spotlight when it correctly predicted that Franklin Roosevelt would be reelected president of the United States. This directly contradicted the well-respected Literary Digest Poll, which had announced that Alfred Landon, governor of Kansas, would not only become president but would win in a landslide. Since then Gallup polls have not simply been a fixture in election polling and analysis; they have also cast light on public opinion regarding a broad variety of social, economic and cultural issues.

Polling results tend to be most noticed during political campaigns or in the wake of important events; during these times, polling provide snapshots of public opinion. This series, however, is more concerned with long-term attitude trends than the response to breaking news. Thus data from many years of Gallup polls are used to trace the evolution of American attitudes. How, for example, have Americans historically viewed immigration? Did attitudes toward foreign newcomers shift during the Great Depression, after the 1941 Japanese attack on Pearl Harbor, or after the terrorist attacks of September 11, 2001? Do opinions on immigration vary across different age, gender, and ethnic groups?

Or, taking another particularly divisive issue treated in this series, what did Americans think about abortion during the many decades the procedure was generally illegal? How has public opinion changed since the Supreme Court's landmark 1973 *Roe v. Wade* decision? How many Americans now favor overturning *Roe*?

By understanding where we as a society have been, we can better understand where we are—and, sometimes, where we are going.

THE WORLD'S LEADER IN SCIENCE AND TECHNOLOGY

As the nineteenth century drew to a close, Charles H. Duell surveyed the incredible advancements in science and technology that were coming to dominate life in the United States and found it hard to imagine further innovation. "Everything that can be invented has been invented," he remarked.

At the time he made that pronouncement, Duell was U.S. commissioner of patents—the federal government official in charge of guiding new inventions into the American marketplace, making them available to consumers while protecting the rights of their inventors. Evidently, Duell observed the technological marvels of the era—the zipper, the motion picture camera, and the vacuum cleaner, among others—and concluded that nothing else could make Americans' daily lives easier.

Duell was, of course, in error. For in 1899, the year in which Duell concluded that technology had reached its limit, some of the era's most

In 1899, the U.S. commissioner of patents, Charles H. Duell (opposite) famously underestimated the potential of future technological innovation. Duell could not imagine developments like jet airliners, nuclear power, and personal computers.

9

brilliant minds were on the verge of making tremendous discoveries that would revolutionize transportation, communications, and other features of American life. And they were doing it for the most part on their own—tinkering in their basements or in backyard sheds, employing crude tools, and using skills they learned as apprentices in machine shops. Far from Duell's field of view, Americans were finding ways to conquer the roadways, the airwaves, and other venues.

Technology has always held an important place in progressive societies. Cultures that have not understood science or developed technology have either collapsed or have doomed their people to dark and backward existences. History is full of such examples. In medieval Europe after the fall of Rome, for example, intellectual advancement drew virtually to a standstill as warring tribes and rulers battled relentlessly for power. Later, during the years of the Inquisition in Europe, religious leaders stifled the work of intellectuals whose teachings seemed to contradict those of the Roman Catholic Church. The Italian astronomer Galileo Galilei is an example of a scientist who suffered the wrath of religious authorities. As the first scientist to direct a telescope toward the heavens, Galileo made many important discoveries, including the fact that there are mountains and craters on the moon. He also discovered the moons of Jupiter and concluded that the Milky Way is composed of stars. But when he stated, accurately, that the earth revolved around the sun—a statement that contradicted biblical teachings of the time—he was imprisoned and his books were burned.

A more extreme case of repression occurred during the 1960s and 1970s in China, when a movement called the Cultural Revolution led to the imprisonment of millions of teachers, scientists, and engineers, as the nation's communist leaders sought to clamp down on ideas that might lead Chinese citizens to demand greater freedoms. When the Cultural Revolution ended

in the late 1970s, the Chinese people found themselves years behind the rest of the world in developing technology and using it to improve their lives.

In the United States, the development of technology and science has generally been encouraged rather than restricted. Still, even in the United States, innovators have always had their doubters. For example, countless people admonished Henry Ford to "get a horse" rather than work on developing his automobile. But Ford persisted. According to David Halberstam's book *The Reckoning*, while showing one of his early cars to a newspaper reporter, he drove by a harness shop and aptly predicted, "His trade is doomed." Ford, for one, could envision an improved future, and, like many other Americans, knew its course would depend greatly on innovation.

Astronomer Galileo Galilei (1564–1642) was tried by the Inquisition and later imprisoned after declaring that the earth revolves around the sun—a true statement, but one that contradicted the official teachings of the Roman Catholic Church at the time.

A U.S. astronaut prepares to step onto the moon, July 1969. The space program was the impetus for many technological developments.

Americans are proud of their country's record in promoting science and technology. In 1959, the Gallup Organization, a national polling institute, asked Americans this question: "Looking ahead ten years, which country do you think will have the leading position in the field of science?" This was not an obvious answer during the late 1950s; at that time, the Soviet Union had beaten the United States into space by launching successful Sputnik satellite missions. America was, more or less, stuck on the ground as it saw its own rocket tests repeatedly explode in fiery failures. Nevertheless, Americans retained the belief that, in the long run, their country would regain the lead over the Russians. Nearly 70 percent of the respondents to the poll said the country leading the world in science in ten years would be the United States.

In 1999, the Gallup Organization asked Americans to name the most important events of the past one hundred years. Their responses enabled Gallup to create a list of eighteen major events. Four of them were based primarily on scientific or technological advancements: Charles Lindbergh's transatlantic flight in 1927; dropping the atomic bomb on the Japanese city of Hiroshima in 1945; the launch of the Sputnik satellites during the 1950s; and the U.S. lunar landing in 1969. Clearly, in many Americans' minds, technological and scientific advancements can be important turning points in history.

2

A SMALLER WORLD: THE AUTOMOBILE, PLANE, TELEPHONE AND RADIO

Although Henry Ford was born and raised on a Michigan farm, as he grew up Ford was much more interested in repairing the rudimentary mechanical devices he found around the home than he was in tilling his father's fields. At the age of 17, Ford left home and walked to the bustling city of Detroit, where he found a job repairing watches. Later he switched careers, and by 1891, at the age of 28, Henry Ford was earning the considerable salary of $100 a month as an engineer for Detroit Edison, the electric company that supplied power to the city. In his spare time, Ford worked on his dream—developing a "horseless carriage."

Henry Ford did not invent the car; in fact, the idea of a self-propelled vehicle had been around for hundreds of years. Both Leonardo da Vinci

Henry Ford's most important contribution to twentieth century technology was not the automobile, which others had developed before him. His factory assembly line, allowing vehicles like the Model T Fords shown on the opposite page to be mass-produced, radically improved the efficiency of American industry.

(1452–1519) and Isaac Newton (1642–1727) theorized that a self-propelled vehicle was possible. In 1769, French engineer Nicolas Joseph Cugnot built a steam-powered device that moved at what was then viewed as an impressive speed for such a vehicle—two-and-a-half miles per hour. (Later, Cugnot drove one of his steam-powered cars into a stone wall, making him the first driver to crash a car.) For decades after Cugnot, resourceful men handy with tools worked on various designs and figured out ways to mount an engine onto a crude chassis and to rig up devices to steer and brake their inventions.

The steam engines used by Cugnot and others were large and awkward. They required a large water boiler and a stockpile of coal and water. Although by the early 20th century some inventors had successfully developed small steam engines for automobiles, it was clear that a car would operate better with a lighter and more dependable source of power. Electric motors held promise. A Scotsman, Robert Anderson, first installed an electric motor onto a carriage in the 1830s. By the 1890s, electric taxis were picking up riders on the streets of New York City.

Other inventors found that a different source of power might work better for the motor vehicle. Since the early 1800s, inventors had experimented with the internal combustion engine: a device that could drive a piston by creating a small controlled explosion inside a metal cylinder. Over the years, inventors would experiment with a variety of fuels for this engine. In 1863, for example, the Belgian engineer Jean Joseph Etienne Lenoir mounted an internal combustion engine powered by oil onto a wagon and drove it 50 miles. Inventors continued to make refinements to the internal combustion engine. In 1885, German engineers Gottlieb Daimler and Wilhelm Maybach invented and patented the first engine that ran on gasoline. The duo built their first automobile in 1889.

MAKING ONE LIKE ANOTHER

Henry Ford built his first car in 1896. He was so engrossed in the project that he failed to notice the car was too big to fit through the door of his shed. He solved that problem by knocking out a brick wall. The car broke down on its maiden voyage, but Ford repaired it and drove home. Four years later, Ford became president of the Detroit Automobile Company, which manufactured cars that could reach the then-impressive speed of 25 miles per hour.

Although Ford did not invent the automobile, he was first to make cars that were not just expensive play-things for the rich. In the early 20th century, there were dozens of car manufacturers headquartered in Detroit. Each company built its cars the same way: a team of tradesmen would work together, fashioning one auto-mobile at a time. A car was usually built to order for the buyer, and a company could make two or three a month. Ford had a much different vision for the process. "The way to make automobiles," he said in 1903, "is to make one automobile like another automobile; just as one pin is like another pin, or one match is like another match when it comes from a match factory."

That year, he established a new business, the Ford Motor Company. Soon he created what would become the first automotive assembly line. Instead of a team of workers laboring over one car at a time, on the assem-bly line each man was assigned a specific, albeit repeti-tive, task to help assemble the car as it moved from one station to another on the factory floor. In its first year of operation, Ford Motor Company produced an amazing 100 cars per month.

In 1908, refinements to Ford's assembly line made it possible to manufacture a car at a much lower cost. The Model T—a simple but sturdy automobile—was devel-oped with the intention that it would be for the average person rather than the rich. "I will build a motor car for the great multitude," Ford declared as the car went into

Henry Ford (1863–1947) said that he wanted to make inexpensive cars that everyone could afford. Millions of people purchased his cars, and other manufacturers incorporated the assembly line concept into their own factories.

production. And the people did respond; eventually, Ford Motor Company sold more than fifteen million Model T's. In its first year of production, it took Ford's workers twelve and one-half hours to produce a single Model T. By 1925, a new Model T rolled off the assembly line every ten seconds.

By then, other manufacturers had adopted Ford's assembly-line techniques. In the late 1920s, more than five million cars a year were being produced by American automakers, most of which were headquartered in Detroit. The growing popularity of automobiles led to the construction of new roads; by 1931, there were more than eight hundred thousand miles of paved roads in America.

However, the stock market crash of 1929, followed by the Great Depression, left many Americans out of work and unable to afford cars. Annual sales of American cars dropped from more than 4.5 million in 1929 to fewer than 2.4 million in 1931. The automakers responded to the dire economic situation by making cars smaller and easier to afford; in fact, General Motors executives considered closing their Cadillac division, which produced large, expensive automobiles for affluent buyers, because during the Depression it was losing money. (Ultimately, however, GM decided to retain the Cadillac division, and today it remains a fixture of the American auto industry.)

By the late 1930s the Depression still gripped Americans, and automakers were still able to sell only 2.5 million cars a year, even though they were making many smaller and cheaper cars. Responding to a

December 1937 Gallup poll, just 63 percent of Americans said they drove automobiles. An even lower number, 59 percent, said they owned cars.

FIRST ATTEMPTS AT FLIGHT

Although the percentage of car owners had fallen, most people had at least ridden in an automobile. The same could not be said for air travel. A 1937 Gallup poll showed that just 33 percent of the respondents had ever flown in an airplane. Many people remained uncertain about the safety of flight. In 1937, the Gallup Organization asked, "If you had your choice, would you prefer to take a long trip by airplane, by train, by automobile, or by bus?" Just 22 percent of the respondents said their preferred mode of travel was airplane. Forty percent said they preferred a train ride, 27 percent said they would take a car, and 5 percent favored the bus.

Although the general public was not very comfortable with planes in 1937, by that time airplane technologies had come a long way. The first plane had actually flown in 1903, when the *Flyer*, built by brothers Wilbur and Orville Wright, lifted off from a sandy hill near Kitty Hawk, North Carolina. Its first flight lasted a mere 12 seconds, covering no more than 120 feet.

As was the case with the automobile, many people's experiments with flight preceeded the Wright brothers' success. In 1783, the Frenchman Jean Pilatre de Rozier made the first tethered hot-air balloon flight; later that year, Pilatre de Rozier, accompanied by the Marquis Francois d'Arlandes, a major in the French army, made the first untethered flight, soaring to an altitude of some 3,000 feet and traveling about 16 miles before coming to a gentle landing just outside Paris.

There was no way to steer the first balloons—they went where the wind took them. Over the next century, engineers would devise ways to add motors to balloons and to steer them by affixing rudimentary rudders. Additionally, engineers experimented with the balloons

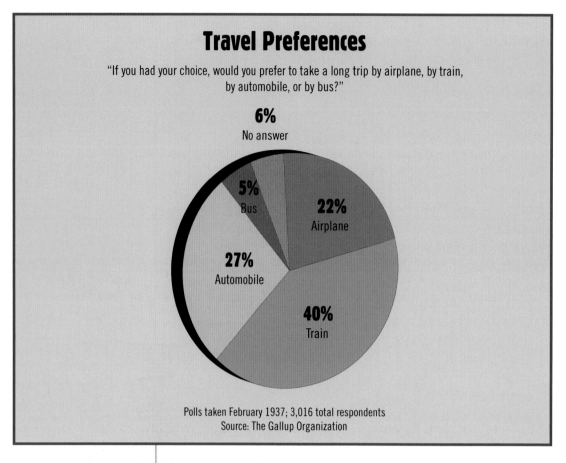

Travel Preferences

"If you had your choice, would you prefer to take a long trip by airplane, by train, by automobile, or by bus?"

6%
No answer

5%
Bus

22%
Airplane

27%
Automobile

40%
Train

Polls taken February 1937; 3,016 total respondents
Source: The Gallup Organization

themselves. For example, an innovation known as the dirigible—a hard shell which held a gas-filled balloon inside—was developed in the 1870s.

Aside from balloons, inventors examined gliders as a flight option as well. In 1853, the British inventor Sir George Cayley designed the first glider that could be piloted by a person; by the end of the century, other inventors had refined Cayley's glider, developing various aircraft that could enable a pilot to be lifted into the air, as long as it was a windy day, by a few friends hoisting the wings high while running as fast as possible.

These developments—motorized balloons and dirigibles and unpowered gliders—were all important steps in the development of self-propelled flight.

However, instead of vehicles that depended on wind or atmospheric currents, the Wrights envisioned a motorized craft that could take off under its own power, fly a pilot to his or her chosen location, and land safely. By 1900 the brothers were experimenting with gliders and concluding that the glider's design was not adaptable for a powered-flight vehicle.

The Wright brothers were not the only ones working on this problem of powered flight. During the late 19th and early 20th centuries, many other inventors experimented with strapping engines and propellers to the front of gliders. However, they all crashed soon after takeoff. The problem was one of control; once in the air, the pilot had no way of steering the apparatus. The Wrights knew they had to resolve this problem and started by studying the anatomy of birds. In doing so, the Wrights realized that birds maintain control while soaring by twisting the tips of their wings. And so the Wrights redesigned the ends of their vehicle's wings, adding stabilizers—flaps that could be controlled, through a series of ropes and pulleys, by the pilot.

What's more, the Wrights realized certain techniques would have to be employed while flying. A motorized aircraft could not make sharp turns, for example. An airplane had to be turned gradually through the method known as banking—leaning the craft slightly to the side so that the plane moves in a gentle curve. The Wrights' early experiments with banking gliders showed that the technique by itself was not the solution, however; the gliders became unstable during the

Brothers Orville and Wilbur Wright were not the first to experiment with human flight, but they were the first to create a successful self-propelled aircraft.

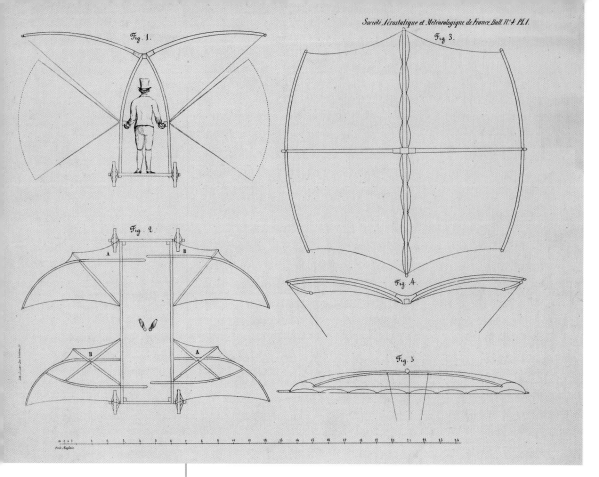

Sir George Cayley drew this design for a self-propelled gliding apparatus in 1853.

maneuver and often crashed. When creating their plane, the Wrights stabilized the aircraft by adding a vertical rudder on the tail. It was a tremendous breakthrough. Today, every airplane achieves altitude and maneuvers through the air using a design based on the principles worked out by Wilbur and Orville Wright in the workroom of their Dayton, Ohio, bicycle shop.

The Wrights decided to use an internal combustion engine to power their craft. When they were unable to find a motor light enough, they designed and built their own. The plane's propellers represented another hurdle. At the time, propellers were designed to churn water and power ships. The Wrights realized, though, that a propeller for an airplane had to be of a far different design. For an airplane to remain airborne, the craft would have to travel at the same speed as the air being moved by the propeller. Therefore, the propeller would have to be large. The Wrights also discovered that using one propeller would cause the plane to spin like a gyroscope. To correct that problem, the Wrights employed two propellers that spun in opposite directions. Each propeller was eight feet long and carved from spruce. As for the plane itself, the *Flyer* was fashioned from ash wood and canvas fabric.

DAWN OF AN ERA

A test of the *Flyer* on December 14, 1903, provided promising results. With Wilbur at the controls, the plane left the ground and remained airborne for three seconds, covering a few dozen feet. The brothers felt encouraged to try again. On the afternoon of December 17, the Wrights prepared to launch their *Flyer* on the sand dunes near Kitty Hawk. They worried about the wind. Kitty Hawk had been selected for the tests because the wind-swept dunes seemed perfect for glider trials. Now, though, the brothers fretted over whether the fragile plane would be able to slice through the gusts. Later, according to *First Flight: The Wright Brothers and the Invention of the Airplane*, Orville would write, "I would hardly think today of making my first flight upon a strange machine in a twenty-seven-mile wind, even if I knew that the machine had already been flown and was safe."

The brothers started the engine, letting it idle for several minutes to warm up. This time, it was Orville's turn to take the controls. He climbed aboard, lying prone in a padded cradle designed for the pilot. He described what happened:

> After running the motor a few minutes to heat it up, I released the wire that held the machine to the track, and the machine started forward into the wind. Wilbur ran at the side of the machine, holding the wing to balance it on the track. Unlike the start on the 14th, made in a calm, the machine, facing a 27-mile wind, started very slowly. Wilbur was able to stay with it till it lifted from the track after a forty-foot run. . . . The course of the

flight up and down was exceedingly erratic, particularly due to the irregularity of the air and partly to lack of experience in handling this machine. The control of the front [stabilizer] was difficult on account of its being balanced too near the center. This gave it a tendency to turn itself when started, so that it turned too far on one side and then too far on the other. As a result, the machine would rise suddenly to about ten feet, and then as suddenly dart for the ground. A sudden dart when a little over a hundred feet from the end of the track, or a little over 120 feet from the point at which it rose into the air, ended the flight.

The first flight lasted 12 seconds. Later that day, the Wrights flew the craft twice more; on the final attempt, Wilbur piloted the *Flyer* for 59 seconds, covering 852 feet. The era of powered flight had commenced.

Soon, other innovators were building planes, although progress was slow. It took until 1908 for a pilot to travel a mile in the air. In 1911, an attempt was made to greatly expand the distance an airplane could fly. A former college football player named Calbraith Perry Rodgers flew across the United States, from Sheepshead Bay, New York, to Long Beach, California. The trip took nearly three months because Rodgers' plane crashed so often. By the time he reached California, a team of mechanics following along on the ground had replaced virtually every component of the plane. Yet despite the slow pace of aviation progress, early inventors realized they were on the cusp of a significant development in the history of human culture. In 1911, aviation pioneer Glenn Martin accurately predicted, "In the near future the airplane will become a thoroughly practical means of transportation for passengers and freight."

The outbreak of World War I provided a boost to the aviation industry. Because the U.S. government recognized that planes could be valuable in battle, it supported their development, and inventors created planes that were more reliable, faster, and more maneuverable. By 1918, some warplanes were fitted with powerful

engines that produced 400 horsepower. (By contrast, the engine of the Wright's original *Flyer* had produced a mere 12 horsepower.)

Improvements in aviation were readily apparent at 7:52 A.M. on May 20, 1927, when the plane S*pirit of St. Louis* lifted off from Roosevelt Field in New York City with Charles Lindbergh at the controls. Thirty-three hours and thirty-two minutes later, Lindbergh's plane landed at Le Bourget Airport near Paris. Lindbergh was the first pilot to make a solo nonstop transatlantic flight. Instantly, Lindbergh became an international hero; his feat proved that a plane carrying passengers and cargo could safely cross thousands of miles of open water without the need to refuel.

(Top) Orville and Wilbur Wright's first flight at Kitty Hawk on December 17, 1903, forever changed the history of transportation. (Inset) The Wright brothers developed an internal combustion engine to power the *Flyer.*

Nevertheless, the public remained wary. By 1939, airline companies were flying routes that connected American cities. Some of them offered transatlantic flights. That year, a Gallup poll asked, "If someone paid your way and you could go, would you be willing to fly across the Atlantic Ocean in one of the new commercial airplanes?" Fifty-five percent of the respondents said no.

"A FAINT SOUND AUDIBLE"

Henry Ford, the Wright brothers, Charles Lindbergh, and the other early pioneers of automobile and airplane transportation helped make the world seem smaller. Their discoveries and innovations enabled a traveler to cover a tremendous distance in a relatively short time.

Truly, though, the world had started appearing smaller long before the twentieth century. In 1844, Samuel Morse had perfected the telegraph and developed the dot-and-dash code that bears his name; with this invention, messages could be sent instantly, as long as two telegraph operators were connected by a wire and each operator understood Morse code.

On March 10, 1876, Alexander Graham Bell made a breakthrough that would revolutionize communications as well. Bell was a teacher of the deaf who in 1872 envisioned a "harmonic telegraph" that would transmit, over wires, not the confusing beeps and hums of Morse code, but audible human language. In 1874, Bell developed the principle of the telephone. Observing how a tiny membrane in the human ear vibrated when hit by sound waves, he theorized that an artificial membrane would likewise vibrate, then relay voice in the

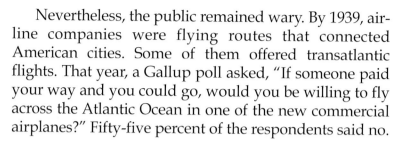

In 1927, Charles Lindbergh became an international celebrity after he piloted the *Spirit of St. Louis* across the Atlantic Ocean. His flight demonstrated to the world that long-distance, nonstop airplane travel was safe.

form of electrical current to a receiver in a remote location. By February 1876, Bell was so optimistic that he was near a breakthrough that he registered his invention, the telephone, with the U.S. Patents Office.

The story is now quite familiar. On March 8, 1876, Bell successfully transmitted the sound of a tuning fork. In his notes he reported, "A faint sound audible," according to the history *Telephone: The First Hundred Years.* Two nights later, Bell and his assistant, Thomas A. Watson, were at work in their shop. They were situated in different rooms, connected by the crudest of telephones. Watson pressed the receiver to his ear, waiting for a sound. Suddenly, Watson heard Bell's voice. The inventor had spilled acid on himself. Watson later recalled, "Almost at once I was astonished to hear Bell's voice . . . distinctly saying, 'Mr. Watson, come here, I want you!' . . . I rushed down the hall into his room and found he had upset the acid of a battery over his clothes."

The telephone quickly came into use. A year after Bell's discovery, a telephone line connected Boston to Somerville, Massachusetts. By 1880, nearly 50,000 people in the United States owned telephones. In 1892, it was possible for a telephone owner in New York to call a friend in Chicago. And by 1936, a Gallup poll reported that 62 percent of American homes were equipped with telephones.

In 1876 Scottish-born inventor Alexander Graham Bell patented his telephone, a device that allowed the spoken word to be transmitted over wires. The telephone soon became widely used; the device pictured here is a model from around 1915.

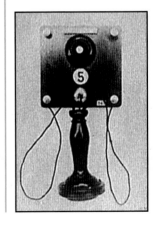

THE DEVELOPMENT OF RADIO

Even more homes had radios—another innovation of the nineteenth century that by the first half of the twentieth century would prove to be invaluable in speeding up communications. Unlike the telephone, the radio required no wires. In 1895, the Italian inventor Guglielmo Marconi transmitted his first "wireless signal" a distance of one mile, making use of a new innovation—the antenna. The development of Marconi's wireless was a significant breakthrough, particularly for the shipping industry, as ships at sea could now communicate with each other, or with stations on land, from a distance.

In the early days of radio, messages were sent in Morse code, but in 1906, the first audible words were transmitted over the radio by Reginald Aubrey Fessenden, a Massachusetts scientist who developed an alternator—a device that speeded up electromagnetic waves into high frequencies capable of carrying human voices over the airwaves. On Christmas eve, Fassenden broadcast a Morse code signal alerting radio owners to prepare for an important announcement. The next sound they heard was a man's voice, followed by a woman singing a song. The broadcast concluded with a violinist playing the hymn, "O Holy Night."

There is no question that the development of the radio sparked a revolution in communications. Two-way radio would become a standard method of communication for the police, the military, pilots, sea captains, and truck drivers. But the radio also sparked a revolution in the entertainment and news industries. Because radio receivers were affordable, they quickly became important vehicles for news. For example, on May 6, 1937, the German dirigible *Hindenburg* exploded in flames and crashed as it was preparing to land in Lakehurst, New Jersey. Millions of listeners heard a live, dramatic description of the tragedy as it unfolded before the

Guglielmo Marconi's "wireless" was the first practical system of communication that used radio waves; as a result, Marconi is often called the "father of radio." The new technology revolutionized twentieth-century communication.

eyes of radio commentator Herb Morrison, who was assigned to cover the airship's arrival:

> It's burst into flames. . . . It is burning, burst into flames and is falling on the mooring mast and all the folks we . . . this is one of the worst catastrophes in the world! . . . Oh, it's four or five hundred feet into the sky, it's a terrific crash ladies and gentlemen . . . oh, the humanity and all the passengers!

That year, a Gallup poll reported that an average of 84 percent of American homes were equipped with radios. Mostly, Americans used their radios for entertainment, because by the 1930s some 63 percent of the programming on American airwaves consisted of music. Among the most popular radio stars of the era were the crooner Rudy Vallee, the comedian Jack Benny, and the ventriloquist Edgar Bergen. Mystery and suspense fans enjoyed programs like *The Shadow*, *The Whistler*, and *Innersanctum*.

Drama was also regularly featured on the radio. Troupes of actors would gather around the microphone in a studio and provide a dramatic reading of a familiar stage play or book. On Halloween night in 1938, the Mercury Theater of the Air, directed by Orson Welles, performed a radio adaptation of *The War of the Worlds*, the 1898 science fiction novel by H.G. Wells that told the story of an invasion of Earth by an army of malevolent Martians. In their adaptation, Welles and the Mercury Theater actors performed the play as though it was a news story unfolding. To some listeners, the broadcast sounded authentic. A Gallup poll taken later that year reported that nearly 4 percent of the show's listeners believed they had heard a real news report and that Martians had actually landed.

3 THE MIRACLE OF TELEVISION

The televised debates between Richard Nixon and John F. Kennedy probably had only a small influence on the outcome of the 1960 presidential election. However, they are generally considered an important moment in the history of television.

As presidential candidates John F. Kennedy and Richard M. Nixon took their places in front of the television cameras on the evening of September 26, 1960, few viewers realized they were about to witness a watershed event not only in the history of American politics but in the history of American television as well. Until that evening, presidential candidates had never debated on national television. In fact, before that time television lacked the stature, influence, and audience to justify a televised presidential debate. Only ten years earlier, the idea of presidential candidates debating on television would have been laughable. In 1950, a Gallup poll reported that just 15 percent of households in the United States even possessed a television.

But things had changed during the 1950s. Following World War II, servicemen returning from the military married their sweethearts, started families, bought homes, and began filling those homes with various consumer products. Suddenly millions of Americans were purchasing cars, refrigerators, washers, dryers, irons, mixers, electric ranges, air conditioners, and televisions. In 1955, the Gallup Organization asked Americans eight times whether they owned television sets; on average, 74 percent of respondents said they did. By 1959, that average had increased to 90 percent of American homes.

The medium of television had significantly advanced during the decade. At first, it had seemed as though television was nothing more than radio with pictures. In the 1930s, radio audiences

Television Trends Over Time

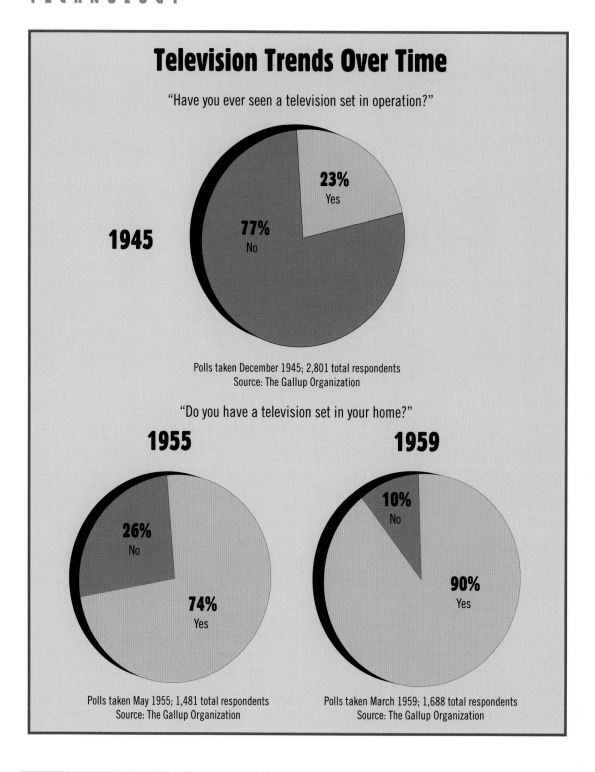

"Have you ever seen a television set in operation?"

1945

23%
Yes

77%
No

Polls taken December 1945; 2,801 total respondents
Source: The Gallup Organization

"Do you have a television set in your home?"

1955

26%
No

74%
Yes

Polls taken May 1955; 1,481 total respondents
Source: The Gallup Organization

1959

10%
No

90%
Yes

Polls taken March 1959; 1,688 total respondents
Source: The Gallup Organization

laughed at the antics of Edgar Bergen and Charlie McCarthy. During the 1950s, the biggest television star in America was Milton Berle, a comic who could always get a laugh by dressing up in women's clothes. Quiz shows easily made the jump from radio to television. So did westerns, dramas, and mysteries.

But the idea that television could provide news and analysis of national or world events took a long time to catch on. One early attempt at providing television viewers with news was the *Today* show on NBC, which debuted in 1952. The show had trouble finding an audience until the producers made a chimpanzee named J. Fred Muggs a regular guest.

Still, the medium would quickly grow up. On March 9, 1954, CBS newsman Edward R. Murrow used his *See It Now* show to unmask communist-hunting Senator Joseph McCarthy of Wisconsin as a charlatan and demagogue who used lies and bluster to ruin the lives and careers of many innocent people. Wrapping up the program, Murrow said:

> This is not the time for men who oppose Senator McCarthy's methods to keep silent. We can deny our heritage and our history, but we cannot escape responsibility for the result. There is no way for a citizen of a republic to abdicate his responsibilities. . . .
>
> The actions of the junior senator from Wisconsin have caused alarm and dismay amongst our allies abroad and given considerable comfort to our enemies, and whose fault is that? Not really his. He didn't create the situation of fear; he merely exploited it, and rather successfully. Cassius was right: "The fault, dear Brutus, is not in our stars but in ourselves."

See It Now helped bring down McCarthy. In January 1954, before the broadcast, a Gallup poll found that 40 percent of the respondents had a favorable opinion of the Wisconsin senator while 35 percent harbored an unfavorable opinion. A week after the *See It Now* broadcast, in a poll taken on March 17, McCarthy's popularity had shifted; by that point, just 32 percent of respondents said they had a favorable opinion of the communist hunter, while nearly 47 percent of the people said they held an unfavorable opinion of McCarthy.

A VISUAL MEDIUM

By the time Kennedy and Nixon stepped before the cameras for their historic debate, television had become a respected outlet for news. Four televised Kennedy-Nixon debates were scheduled for that fall; ABC broadcast two, while CBS and NBC each broadcast one. The one that is remembered most in history is the first, which was staged at a studio in Chicago.

In the weeks leading up to the debate, there was interest in the event. A Gallup poll reported in late August that 55 percent of Americans claimed to have "a lot of interest" in watching the upcoming debates. That number would increase as the date of the first debate drew closer.

Vice President Nixon arrived at the television studio first, about an hour before the debate was scheduled to begin. For twenty-four hours prior to the debate, Nixon had kept up a grueling schedule. He had campaigned heavily, slept little, and spent several hours that afternoon preparing for the televised forum, filling his head with facts and figures. Kennedy, in contrast, spent the day relaxing at his Chicago hotel, even taking some time to lounge in the sun on the hotel roof. When he arrived at the television studio, the senator from Massachusetts looked relaxed and tanned.

Kennedy understood the value of television and realized that much of its effect comes from the fact that it is a visual medium. Nixon, however, seemed not to recognize this. He ignored his advisors' warning that harsh television lights tend to make people look pale and that he should spend time in the makeup chair. Kennedy received the same warning from his aides; unlike Nixon, he took the aides' advice.

That night, viewers tuned in and saw a simple set with Kennedy and Nixon standing behind podiums. A panel of journalists was to ask the questions, while veteran television newsman Howard K. Smith moderated the broadcast.

During the debate, the candidates fielded the same questions they had answered many times before. Neither candidate announced a new position, stated a historic declaration, or made a verbal blunder. For the first time, though, it became clear that the medium was as important as the message. The hot television lights made the sweat bead on Nixon's forehead and upper lip. Because he had refused pancake makeup, the stubble from his five o'clock shadow showed under the glare, making him look haggard. In contrast, Kennedy looked youthful, relaxed, suntanned, and clean-shaven.

John F. Kennedy was among the first politicians to recognize the power of television, and often used the medium to his advantage.

He stood at ease in front of the cameras. According to historian Theodore White's book *The Making of the President 1960*, Kennedy's media advisor, J. Leonard Reinsch, looked at the image of the two opponents on his television and said, "Every time we get these two fellows on the screen side by side, we're going to gain and he's going to lose."

In the weeks preceding the debate, several Gallup polls had shown Nixon and Kennedy running in a virtual dead heat in the campaign. Following the first debate, a Gallup poll reported that Kennedy's performance had gained him a three-point lead, although it would turn out to be temporary. Gallup also estimated that some 64 million Americans watched the debate on television—an unprecedented audience for the era.

Indeed, the audience size is even more impressive when one considers that in 1960, the number of American homes with televisions stood at 40 million—meaning that not only were most sets in America tuned to the debate that night but that whole families gathered around and watched the event together.

Americans who watched the debate on television told a Gallup poll that in their minds, Kennedy won the first debate. A total of 44 percent of the respondents said Kennedy did a better job in the debate than Nixon, whose performance was rated higher by 23 percent of the respondents. (Surprisingly, polls showed that those who listened to the debate on the radio believed that

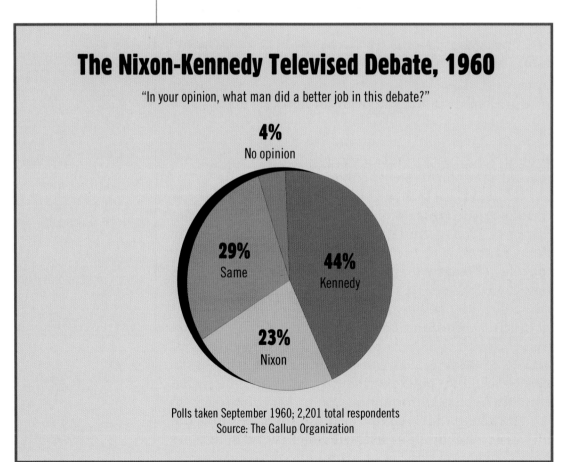

The Nixon-Kennedy Televised Debate, 1960

"In your opinion, what man did a better job in this debate?"

4%
No opinion

29%
Same

44%
Kennedy

23%
Nixon

Polls taken September 1960; 2,201 total respondents
Source: The Gallup Organization

Nixon had done a better job.) Kennedy's performance in the debate undoubtedly helped him six weeks later, when the senator from Massachusetts scored a razor-thin victory over Nixon in the November election.

Today, presidential debates are routinely broadcast on national television. Media advisors working for the major candidates spend months planning the telecasts down to the tiniest of details, such as the camera angles and the podium heights—all so their candidate isn't portrayed in a less-than-flattering light and doesn't suffer a fate similar to Nixon's in 1960.

MANIPULATING ELECTRONS

The word television, a compound of the Greek *tele* ("far off") and Latin *vision* ("to see"), was first used in a 1907 issue of *Scientific American* magazine. A method of transmitting photographs over telegraph lines had just been developed, and scientists wondered whether it would also be possible to transmit moving pictures.

The first attempts to do this involved mechanical devices. In 1884, the German inventor Paul Nipkow developed a perforated mechanical wheel that could relay and project an image while spinning. For the next three decades, inventors experimented with the Nipkow disk, trying unsuccessfully to adapt it to the electronic transmission of images.

In rural Utah during the early 1920s, a fifteen-year-old farm boy named Philo Farnsworth was proving himself to be something of a scientific genius. As a high school freshman, Farnsworth excelled so far ahead of the other students in his science class that his teacher, Justin Tolman, accepted him into a chemistry class with seniors. Soon, Farnsworth was outperforming the seniors as well, and Tolman found himself giving private tutoring lessons to Farnsworth.

The notion that images could be transmitted over the airwaves had always fascinated Farnsworth, and he would often discuss the concept with Tolman. In 1922,

Tolman walked into his classroom to find Farnsworth busy at the blackboard, writing equations and sketching schematics. When Tolman asked his student the meaning of the equations, Farnsworth answered that he had developed an idea for television. According to *The Boy Genius and the Mogul: The Untold Story of Television*, Farnsworth told his teacher, "It can't be done by mechanical means. I propose to do it by wholly electronic means, by manipulating electrons."

Farnsworth's plan called for development of a vacuum tube that would feature an interior light-sensitive surface. The tube would react to light and dark areas of the object placed before it, converting its image to electrical impulses. That tube would be the camera. The impulses would then be transmitted—either by wire or over the airwaves—to a receiver, which would convert the electrical impulses back to light.

Farnsworth showed Tolman a photograph from a newspaper, pointing out the process printers use to reproduce a picture on the printed page, in which the photograph is reproduced using dots of various shadings. Farnsworth believed a similar process could be employed to transmit moving images electronically. He told Tolman:

> If you had a reading glass you would see that this picture is made up of many small dots. There are probably 250,000 dots in such a reproduction. To transmit a picture of like quality over television, each of these dots must be picked up separately and sent in sequence. To fool the eye, all this must be done in a fraction of a second. To get smooth motion as in motion pictures, we must probably send the pictures at a rate of thirty a second. In other words, to do the thing successfully we must register and transmit 250,000 variations every thirtieth of a second. That means something like 7,500,000 changes in intensity every second.

Farnsworth knew that no mechanical wheel could spin fast enough to convert the images. Instead, Farnsworth believed his vacuum tube, which he called an "image dissector," could break down the image into dots and send them, line by line, to a television receiver.

Five years later, Philo Farnsworth headed a research lab in San Francisco. On September 27, 1927, he successfully transmitted a television image from one room of his lab to another. It wasn't much of a show—he had simply transmitted the image of a rotating black square with a line etched across the center. Nevertheless, after Farnsworth transmitted the image, he turned to a group of his investors and said, "There you are, electronic television."

By then, Farnsworth and some of the nation's largest corporations were in a race to develop television. The Radio Corporation of America (RCA), for example,

Scientist Philo T. Farnsworth, the first to electronically transmit an image, poses with an early television set in 1929. It took decades for television to reach a wide audience, because the first sets were very expensive and there was little regular programming available.

made a big investment in developing the new technology. As early as 1923, RCA General Manager David Sarnoff wrote in a memorandum, "I believe that television, which is the technical name for seeing instead of hearing by radio, will come to pass in due course."

SLOW TO CATCH ON

Nevertheless, even after a working television was developed, it would be decades before television ownership would be widespread. Few people could afford televisions, especially during the Great Depression—a modestly priced set that featured a four-by-five-inch screen sold for $200. In addition, the programming was sporadic. Occasionally, the owner of a television could pick up a broadcast of a boxing match or a politician's speech, but most talented performers were on radio at the time.

Still, the future of television looked bright. At the 1939 World's Fair in New York, RCA's pavilion was devoted to the advances in this new mode of communications. "This miracle of engineering skills which one day will bring the world to the home also brings a new American industry to serve man's material welfare. Television will become an important factor in American economic life," Sarnoff predicted.

However, the outbreak of World War II slowed the development of television. The nation's top engineers and scientists were asked to contribute to the war effort by developing weapons and other military technologies, leaving few scientists to concentrate on television and other consumer products.

Soon after the war ended, though, many American corporations devoted their resources to television projects. They aimed to sell televisions to the American consumers—even though at that point, these consumers weren't all that sure they wanted sets in their homes. In late 1945, just 23 percent of respondents told Gallup they had even seen a television in operation. As a follow-up question, the poll asked respondents how long it would take before half the people in their communities owned television sets. The largest number of people—nearly 29 percent—thought it would take ten years for that to happen.

WIRED FOR CABLE

By the time Nixon and Kennedy debated, there were three major television networks: ABC, NBC, and CBS. Today, of course, those three networks still exist, but there are now many independent television stations as well as hundreds of channels available on cable and satellite services.

The history of cable television dates back to the late 1940s, when television owners in rural and mountainous areas found they couldn't pick up signals transmitted from the television stations, which were typically located in big cities. Some television owners found that if they wired their sets together, however, and connected them to one tall antenna, their reception improved immensely. Entrepreneurs saw the commercial potential of cable. They erected tall antennas and started charging fees to homeowners to hook up.

In the late 1950s, the number of cable subscribers across the United States could be counted in the hundreds. By the 1970s, though, major corporations saw the programming possibilities of cable. Instead of merely picking up the network transmissions and relaying them to cable subscribers, the cable companies would also provide programming not available on network television. Viewers who paid subscription fees could view live sporting events as well as movies that were uncut by network censors and uninterrupted by commercials. Because the cable signals were not on the public airwaves, cable programmers could avoid editing feature films in order to comply with decency standards adopted by the Federal Communications Commission. The cable company owners believed their programming would encourage people to subscribe.

The Advent of Cable TV

"Have you heard or read anything about cable TV?"

4%
Don't know/no answer

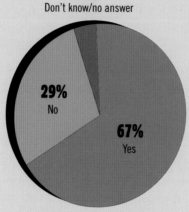

29%
No

67%
Yes

Polls taken March 1971; 1,619 total respondents
Source: The Gallup Organization

"If cable TV made it possible for you to receive clearer pictures of the shows that appear on regular TV channels, and also receive without commercial interruptions movies, sports events, and other specials not available on regular TV, would you be willing or unwilling to subscribe to it for a minimum charge of $5 to $8 a month?"

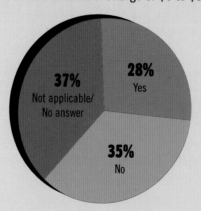

37%
Not applicable/
No answer

28%
Yes

35%
No

Polls taken March 1971; 1,619 total respondents
Source: The Gallup Organization

People caught on slowly. In 1971, a Gallup poll reported that just 67 percent of Americans were aware of cable television and what it offered. The poll also asked people whether they would be willing to pay a monthly fee of five dollars or eight dollars to subscribe to a cable service, if it meant they could be assured of clear reception as well as access to uncut and uninterrupted movies, sporting events, and other programming not available on the networks. Although 28 percent of respondents said they would be willing to pay those fees, 35 percent said they wouldn't.

By the 1980s, cable had spread to far more homes, thanks largely to the establishment of specialized channels—for example, ESPN for the sports fan, AMC for lovers of old movies, CNN for news junkies, and MTV for teenagers. MTV (Music Television), which showed music videos, was born in 1981. In MTV's first year of operation, the channel was in the homes of 2.5 million cable subscribers. Two years later, 17 million homes were subscribing to cable networks. The success of MTV and the other specialty channels helped spread cable television across the country. In 1995, the Gallup poll reported that nearly 73 percent of American homes were wired for cable.

HOME RECORDING

During the late 1940s and early 1950s, many television shows were performed live. Viewers at home saw live performances by comedians such as Ernie Kovacs and Sid Caesar. When singers, musicians, and jugglers tried out their acts on programs like *The Original Amateur Hour*, they gave live performances. Although some programs were recorded on movie film, this was an expensive process and therefore was rarely done by the networks. However, during the 1950s a process for recording sounds and images on inexpensive magnetic videotape was developed. By the 1960s, videotaping had become standard practice at all the television networks.

A 1978 advertisement for an early videocassette recorder, which cost nearly $1,000. During the 1980s, as the price of VCRs dropped, more Americans purchased the devices for their homes.

In the 1970s, two Japanese electronics companies—Sony Corporation and Victor Company of Japan, or JVC—introduced videotaping to the home consumer market. With this innovation, people could shoot home movies on videotape rather than on 8 mm film. Or, by hooking up videocassette recorders (VCRs) to their television sets, they could record their favorite programs. A VCR could even be preset, so that it could automatically start recording at a certain time—meaning that people did not have to be home to record. As a result, there was no reason to rush home from a child's baseball game to catch a favorite television program, or to stay up past bedtime to watch a favorite movie. Instead, people could record the programs and watch them at their leisure.

Entrepreneurs soon began to make deals with Hollywood studios, so that films would be available on videotape soon after they were shown in theaters. People could then buy movies or, more commonly, rent them for a few days from the neighborhood video store. By the 1990s, advances in computer technology enabled entrepreneurs to add another format to the home video market: digital video discs, or DVDs. Similar to compact discs that play music, DVDs provide a clearer image than videotape and can even be played on home computers equipped with DVD drives. In 2001, a Gallup poll found that 76 percent of Americans owned a videocassette recorder or DVD player, and that nearly 24 percent of Americans owned both.

CHANGING TV TECHNOLOGY

Television has come a long way since Philo Farnsworth diagrammed his ideas for an image dissector on a high school blackboard. There is no question, though, that innovators are continually finding ways to change how Americans enjoy television.

One recent innovation that is growing more popular is digital video recorders (DVR), such as TiVo. These devices use powerful computers and sophisticated software to record television programs onto a hard drive for later viewing. DVRs were first introduced to consumers in 1999.

In recent years, high-definition television (HDTV) has become available to American consumers. Back in 1922, Farnsworth envisioned the dots in a television image transmitted line by line. That is exactly how the image is transmitted, with most television sets today receiving 525 lines of data. In HDTV, up to twice as many lines of information are transmitted. As a result, the dots in each line are smaller and more tightly compacted and capable of producing a spectrum of more than 16 million variations of colors. HDTV viewers can therefore see detail unimagined nearly a century ago when television pioneers first envisioned transmitting moving pictures over the airwaves.

4

THE RACE FOR SPACE

It was the size of a beach ball and weighed just 184 pounds. Its only function was the transmission of a "beep" every three-tenths of a second. And yet on October 4, 1957, when the Soviet Union launched Sputnik, the world changed forever.

Sputnik—a Russian word for "traveling companion"—was the first artificial satellite successfully launched into Earth's orbit. Its launch marked the beginning of the space age, and also the beginning of the space race. For the next 92 days Sputnik passed overhead, eventually orbiting the Earth 1,400 times before burning to a cinder from the friction of reentry into the atmosphere. It had beeped hundreds of thousands of times. According to *Sputnik: The Shock of the Century*, an NBC radio announcer told his audience to "listen now for the sound that forevermore separates the old from the new."

The beeping sound signaled to Americans that they had fallen behind the Soviets in the development of space technology. This was a frightening position during the Cold War, in

(Opposite) The enormous Saturn V rocket, carrying the Apollo 11 capsule, lifts off from Cape Canaveral, Florida, in June 1969. The successful Apollo 11 moon landing would cap a decade-long "space race" between the United States and Soviet Union.

which the U.S. and Soviet Union were striving for global superiority. U.S. leaders did not want the Soviets to have any threatening advantage.

Less than a month after Sputnik's launch, the Soviets sent Sputnik II into orbit. The second satellite weighed 1,100 pounds and outdid its predecessor, staying in orbit for 150 days and circling Earth 2,370 times. The satellite also carried a passenger—a dog named Laika, proving that living creatures could survive the rigors of a rocket launch as well as the weightless environment of space. Laika gave its life for the mission—the unfortunate animal died because the Soviets had no way to bring the dog home. Nevertheless, the mission was a tremendous engineering triumph. The Soviet news agency Tass boasted, "Artificial earth satellites will pave the way to interplanetary travel, and apparently our contemporaries will witness how the freed and conscientious labor of the people of the new socialist society makes the most daring dreams of mankind a reality."

Americans could not immediately match the Soviets' accomplishments in space. On December 6, 1957, while both Sputniks soared overhead, the U.S. Navy attempted to launch a satellite into space. The rocket exploded on the launch pad. Two months later, the Army successfully sent the satellite Explorer I into orbit. The most significant accomplishment of Explorer I was the discovery of the Van Allen radiation belts that circle the Earth. However, when the American military attempted two more launches in early 1958, both ended in fiery and dismal failures.

Many Americans were disturbed by the Russian successes and American failures. One was Senator Lyndon B. Johnson, who would later become president and would champion the American space program. In a NASA history titled "Sputnik and the Origins of the Space Age," Johnson recalled his reaction when Sputnik was launched. "Now, somehow, in some new way, the sky seemed almost alien," he said. "I also remember the profound shock of realizing that it might be possible for another nation to achieve technological superiority over this great country of ours."

COMPLACENT VIEW

Other Americans were just as profoundly shocked. On October 2, 1958, just before the first anniversary of the Sputnik I launch, a Gallup poll found that 41 percent of Americans believed the Soviets were ahead of the United States in missiles and rocket science; at the same time, however, 37 percent of respondents felt America was in the lead. Wrote pollster George Gallup:

> When the Russians launched their man-made 'moon' one year ago this Sunday, it shocked America out of the complacent view that the U.S. was ahead of the Soviets in all departments.
>
> Ever since October 5 of last year the debate sparked by Sputnik I has raged—and centered chiefly on the question of which of the two giants in the East-West struggle—the U.S. or Russia—has the lead in different fields. . . . By a slim margin, Americans concede that the Russians have the edge on the U.S. in the field of missiles and rockets.

Americans would make an effort to catch up. Following the early launch pad disasters, President Dwight D. Eisenhower took the responsibility for the space program out of the hands of the military. In 1958 he established the National Aeronautics and Space Administration (NASA) and put it in charge of overseeing a program in which humans would travel in space.

Eisenhower's successor, President John F. Kennedy, was an enthusiastic supporter of the space program as well. On May 25, 1961, just days after NASA launched its first successful manned mission into space—a brief, suborbital flight by astronaut Alan B. Shepard Jr.—Kennedy proposed an even greater challenge, a mission to the moon. Speaking before a joint session of Congress, Kennedy charged, "This nation should commit itself to achieving the goal, before this decade is out, of landing a man on the moon, and returning him safely to Earth. No single space project will be more important to mankind or more important for the long-range exploration of space; and none will be so difficult or expensive to accomplish."

Kennedy's words stirred enthusiasm for the space program among Americans. Yet three weeks before Shepard had made his modest flight, the Soviet cosmonaut Yuri Gagarin actually had become the first man in space. Not only had he been first, but he had made a much more impressive flight than Shepard's because his spacecraft had orbited the Earth.

Although the United States was still behind, many Americans didn't see it that way. Regardless of the Russian accomplishments, two weeks after Kennedy issued his challenge, a Gallup poll reported that Americans believed, by a margin of 49 percent to 30 percent, that the United States was ahead in the area of long-range missiles and rockets. Gallup reported, "Russia's recent achievements in space have not shaken the American public's confidence. . . . If anything—in a Gallup Poll conducted since our own successful man-in-space shot—optimism about U.S. leadership in the missile race has increased since the first of the year."

For Americans, there would be many triumphs ahead as their country raced the Soviets to the moon and beyond. But there would also be many tragedies. Along the way, the public would not always be supportive.

PASSING THE SOVIETS

The rockets that would one day carry humans into space had their origins in experiments conducted nearly four decades before President Kennedy disclosed his plans for a moon landing. In March 1926, Robert Hutchings Goddard, a professor of physics at Clark University in Massachusetts, successfully launched a liquid-propellant

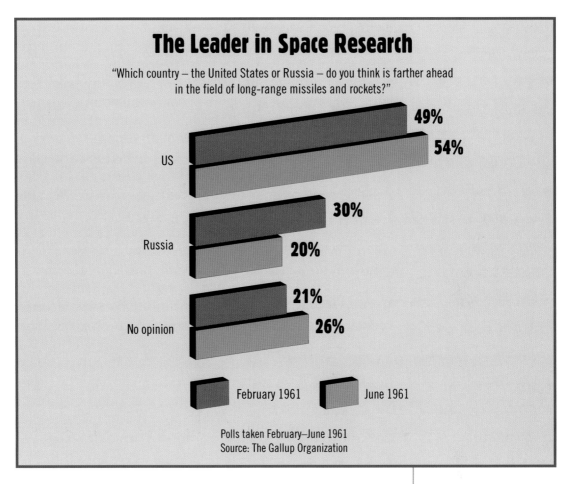

The Leader in Space Research

"Which country – the United States or Russia – do you think is farther ahead in the field of long-range missiles and rockets?"

US: 49%, 54%

Russia: 30%, 20%

No opinion: 21%, 26%

February 1961   June 1961

Polls taken February–June 1961
Source: The Gallup Organization

rocket into the sky. It reached an altitude of 41 feet and traveled just 184 feet. The same principles that Goddard used to fire a tiny rocket from a field on his Aunt Effie's farm were employed years later by the engineers who designed NASA's enormous rockets.

Although Goddard's rockets grew larger and his achievements grew more impressive, the next major leap in space technology was accomplished far from America's shores and under far more sinister circumstances. By 1933 Adolf Hitler's Nazi Party had taken power in Germany, and Hitler recognized the military possibilities of rockets. Hitler learned about the work of a group of students and engineers who called

German rocket scientist Wernher von Braun (1912–1977) helped develop the U.S. missile program after the Second World War. He joined NASA when the agency was created in 1958, and is considered an important pioneer in the exploration of space.

themselves the Verein für Ramschiffahrt—the German Society for Space Travel. The society, which included a young engineer named Wernher von Braun, had been experimenting with rockets. Hitler placed the resources of the Nazi regime at the disposal of the young German rocket scientists, and eventually built the $100 million Peenemünde rocket base on the Baltic coast.

The rocket program played no role in the early years of World War II, which started when Germany invaded Poland in September 1939. Initially, Germany was able to conquer many neighboring countries, including France, and for a time it seemed that all Europe might fall under Hitler's control. However, by 1944 the tide of the war had turned, and American, British, and Russian forces were liberating the conquered countries of Europe. It was at this point that the rocket scientists at Peenemünde provided Hitler's regime with a final ray of hope. The devastating V-1 and V-2 rockets, filled with explosives, were aimed at London, destroying thousands of homes and other buildings and killing more than 11,000 British civilians and servicemen. The V-2 was particularly devastating; it was 46 feet tall, weighed some 27,000 pounds, and could travel 500 miles in just a few minutes.

Fortunately for the Allies, the war was all but over by the time the V-2 was perfected. In early 1945, von Braun, then the head of the German rocket program, decided it would be better to surrender to the Americans than the Soviets. He led 500 German scientists out of Peenemünde, where they surrendered to a U.S. Army unit. They also turned over to their captors records, plans, parts, and entire V-2 rockets. The Americans, seeing the value of capturing the entire German rocketry program virtually intact, shipped the rockets as well as the scientists back to the United States, where they were put to work developing a U.S. missile program. But the Soviets captured their own V-2 rockets, and they, too, found themselves privy to details of the work that had been accomplished at Peenemünde.

America's next step forward in the space race occurred over a remote desert in California on the morning of October 14, 1947, when test pilot Chuck Yeager flew the experimental X-1 rocket plane faster than the speed of sound. The flight was a tremendous engineering accomplishment because many people had believed it was physically impossible for humans to travel that fast. Breaking the sound barrier was an important psychological step, but a trip into space was still out of the question. Yeager's plane had gone more than 750 miles an hour, but to break the grip of Earth's gravity and achieve orbit, a rocket would have to travel more than 24,000 miles an hour.

By the early 1950s, Americans were warming up to the idea of space travel. At the movies, Americans could see such Hollywood dramatizations as *Destination Moon*, *Forbidden Planet*, and *When Worlds Collide*—all suggesting that space travel was in their future. Walt Disney's weekly television show aired a series of documentaries on space travel, the first of which was titled *Man in Space*. Disney featured Wernher von Braun in the documentaries, and the rocket scientist also served as technical advisor to the productions. In late 1954 and early 1955, a Gallup poll asked Americans whether they would like to ride a rocket to the moon. Nearly 9 percent of the respondents said yes.

In the early 1960s, America's space pioneers got very serious about the race to the moon. Following Shepard's suborbital flight, NASA launched five more of the so-called Mercury missions. During the third mission, astronaut John Glenn became the first American to orbit the earth. Next came the Gemini program. Two astronauts, sitting side by side, were launched into orbit, where they spent several days rehearsing the maneuvers and testing the technology that would be employed for the moon missions. In 1966, after ten manned flights, the Gemini program ended and NASA prepared for the next phase of the space race, the Apollo program—which had the goal of reaching the moon.

Americans believed the accomplishments of the Gemini program had far outpaced the Soviet efforts in space; in 1965, amid a string of successful Gemini flights, nearly 47 percent of respondents to a Gallup poll said they believed the United States held the edge in the space race, compared to 24 percent of respondents who said the Soviets were in the lead.

Perhaps, though, the Americans had moved too quickly. On the afternoon of January 27, 1967, during a routine test of the Apollo 1 capsule's instruments, fire erupted in the cockpit of the spacecraft when a spark from a poorly insulated wire ignited the capsule's pure oxygen atmosphere. Three American astronauts lost their lives—the first American astronauts to die.

Americans were shocked and saddened by the tragedy. For years, they had been wildly enthusiastic about the space race. Suddenly, that enthusiasm cooled. A month after the tragedy, 61 percent of respondents to a Gallup

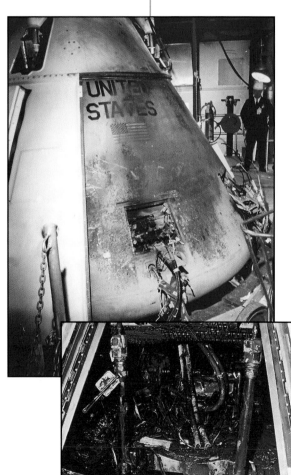

poll said they did not feel a moon mission was important; just 33 percent said they felt it was still important to beat the Soviets to the moon.

"THE EAGLE HAS LANDED"

Despite Americans' sentiments, NASA forged ahead. Over the next 21 months, the Apollo capsule was redesigned to make it safer. Wiring was rerouted and better insulated, and the capsule's atmosphere was changed to a less volatile mix of oxygen and nitrogen. After several test missions that included Earth orbits as well as a trial run into lunar orbit, a mission to land on the moon was scheduled to launch in July of 1969. It appeared certain that NASA would achieve President Kennedy's goal of landing a man on the moon before the end of the decade.

To break the pull of Earth's gravity, the three-man Apollo space capsule as well as the landing craft, known as the lunar module, would have to be boosted into space atop the 363-foot-tall Saturn V rocket. The rocket provided 7.5 million pounds of thrust—equivalent to 180 million horsepower. Forty-three years after Robert Goddard had first experimented with tiny rockets on his aunt's farm, the gargantuan Saturn V was rolled onto its launch pad at Cape Canaveral in Florida.

On July 16, 1969, the Apollo 11 spacecraft lifted off for its historic mission. Aboard were three astronauts—Neil Armstrong, Edwin Aldrin, and Michael Collins. After reaching lunar orbit, Armstrong and Aldrin would climb aboard the lunar module, named *Eagle*, leaving Collins behind in the command module *Columbia* to circle the moon and await the return of the landing craft.

Apollo 11 entered lunar orbit on July 20. During the twelfth lunar orbit, Armstrong and Aldrin took their places aboard *Eagle* and descended to the moon, aiming for a landing in the Sea of Tranquility, a vast plain on the moon where it was believed *Eagle* would be able to find a safe landing zone. A short time later, Armstrong's words to Mission Control in Houston, Texas, were heard by hundreds of millions of people watching the television news coverage of the landing: "Houston, Tranquility Base here. The *Eagle* has landed."

Six-and-a-half hours later, Armstrong eased himself out of the *Eagle*'s hatch and slowly descended the ladder to the surface of the moon. NASA had equipped *Eagle* with a black-and-white television camera, which Armstrong activated prior to his trip down the ladder. On Earth, an estimated audience of 600 million people—a quarter of the world's population—watched the grainy television picture as Armstrong and then Aldrin took man's first steps on the moon.

The Apollo 11 astronauts returned to Earth as heroes. The space program again enjoyed widespread support among the American people; a few months after the lunar landing, 18 percent of respondents to a Gallup poll said they believed there would even be human colonies on the moon within 20 years.

While that would not happen, other advancements were made. After the conclusion of the Apollo program in 1972, NASA shifted its manned space flight emphasis to the Space Shuttle program and, later, to the establishment of the permanent International Space Station that remains in orbit around Earth.

As it turned out, the Soviets never got close to landing a manned mission on the moon. Plagued by engineering difficulties, the Soviets limited their space program to missions in Earth's orbit. Then, following the breakup of the Soviet Union in 1991, the Russians became partners with Americans in creating the International Space Station, a development that never would have been anticipated in the years of the intense space-race competition. Both countries have participated in several joint missions to pursue scientific and commercial applications for the Space Station. Today, the work aboard the Space Station rarely garners the

Apollo 11 astronauts Neil Armstrong, Michael Collins, and Buzz Aldrin pose in their spacesuits before their historic mission. On July 20, 1969, some 600 million people watched as Armstrong and Aldrin took the first steps on the moon. In all, twelve Americans would explore the lunar surface before the Apollo program ended in the mid-1970s.

headlines that the Apollo astronauts could expect some four decades ago. Still, the American people harbor very strong feelings about the space program, and those feelings often have intensified when tragedies have occurred.

RETURN TO SPACE

The space shuttle is a reusable spacecraft that is launched into orbit with the help of two boosters that disengage and then return to Earth during the shuttle's ascent. At the completion of its mission, the shuttle reenters the atmosphere and glides in for a landing, touching down as any airplane would land. The first shuttle mission was launched in 1981. Since then, NASA's fleet of shuttles has flown dozens of times.

Twice, though, tragedy has struck the shuttle fleet. On January 28, 1986, the shuttle *Challenger* exploded 73 seconds after takeoff, when an engineering flaw in one of the boosters caused the fuel to ignite. Seven crew members were killed in the accident, including the school teacher Christa McAuliffe, who had been picked to be the first civilian to fly in space. The second tragedy occurred on February 1, 2003, when the shuttle *Columbia* disintegrated over Texas as it was gliding in for a landing in Florida. The accident was blamed on faulty tiles on the outside of the shuttle, which were supposed to protect the spacecraft from the heat of reentry. All seven astronauts on board were killed.

After both accidents, Americans renewed their dedication to the space program. In 1986, following the *Challenger* accident, a Gallup poll found 79 percent of Americans committed to the shuttle program. In 2003, shortly after the *Columbia* accident, 49 percent of respondents said they wanted the federal government to maintain funding for the space program, while 25 percent of respondents said they would like to see funding increased. Both polls showed Americans rallying behind the space program in times of crises. Indeed, even with the deaths of the seven *Columbia* astronauts still fresh in their minds, 30 percent of the respondents said they would like to fly in space aboard the space shuttle. In contrast, in 1999—a time between the two accidents when space flight had become something of a mundane accomplishment—24 percent of respondents to a Gallup poll said they wanted to see funding for space missions decreased, while 10 percent of respondents said they hoped the federal government would terminate the space program.

Despite the varying support of public opinion, the space program continues. Two years after the *Columbia* accident, NASA re-launched the shuttle program. Additionally, the space agency has made many important scientific achievements with unmanned spacecrafts, sending probes to other planets to investigate atmospheric and surface conditions while beginning a rudimentary search for life on other worlds. In other developments, some Americans have found a way to reach space on their own without becoming

Spending for the Space Program

"Do you think spending on the U.S. space program should be increased, kept at the present level, reduced, or ended altogether?"

10%
Ended altogether

1%
Don't know

16%
Increased

24%
Reduced

1999 Opinions

49%
Kept at present level

Polls taken December 1999; 536 total respondents
Source: The Gallup Organization

7%
Ended altogether

2%
Don't know

25%
Increased

17%
Reduced

2003 Opinions

49%
Kept at present level

Polls taken February 2003; 1,000 total respondents
Source: The Gallup Organization

The space shuttle *Discovery* blasts off in July 2005. *Discovery*'s mission, during which the shuttle visited the International Space Station, was the first after the February 2003 *Columbia* disaster.

NASA-trained astronauts. In 2004, the privately financed SpaceShipOne reached an altitude of some 60 miles—a distance high enough to qualify as space. The flight marked the first time a manned craft that was designed, built, and flown by civilians broke the barriers of Earth's gravity. When the ship's designer, Burt Rutan, was asked what inspired him to reach for space, he recalled watching television in the 1950s as Wernher von Braun explained the mysteries of space travel on Walt Disney's documentaries. In a BBC article, he explained, "The most exciting thing I saw as a child was this vision of von Braun going to the back of the Moon. That was the strongest impression of adventure, and I think that was so important because the whole world had that sense of adventure 500 years ago when Magellan made it around the world."

Americans have benefited greatly from the technological developments associated with the space program. The demands of space travel required advancements in computer technology and automation, and new developments in energy management, construction and manufacturing technology, and other areas. Today, many NASA-inspired products—from aluminum foil and no-stick pans to powerful computers—are used in every home.

5

THE ATOMIC AGE

By the summer of 1958, the Soviet Union's success with Sputnik, contrasted with America's fiery failures on the launch pad, caused many people to doubt whether the United States truly did hold a technological advantage over the rest of the world. In early August, the U.S. Navy provided reassurance of America's technological strength when the submarine *Nautilus* sailed beneath the North Pole, covering some 1,800 miles underwater. This was a feat that until then had never been possible; *Nautilus* was able to accomplish it because the submarine was powered by a nuclear reactor. Because of this, it was capable of covering tremendous distances and remaining submerged for months. Americans greeted the news of the achievement with no small degree of relief. Shortly after the trip took place, Senate Republican Leader William F. Knowland of California remarked to the Senate, "This should give us courage and remind us to have faith. It shows that this is no time to sell America short."

While the *Nautilus* was making its way under the pole, plans were already on the table

The atomic age began on August 6, 1945, when the U.S. bomber *Enola Gay* dropped an atomic bomb on Hiroshima, Japan, killing an estimated 80,000 civilians.

63

to further enhance the power of nuclear-powered sub-marines. As a result, in 1959, the nuclear submarine *George Washington* made its maiden voyage equipped with sixteen Polaris missiles. Each missile carried a nuclear warhead in its nose cone. Now, American nuclear submarines could destroy a city or other target virtually anywhere in the world. After the nuclear sub *Ethan Allen* successfully test-fired a Polaris missile high above the Pacific Ocean on May 6, 1962, the editors of *Navy Times* wrote, "Polaris obviously has rewritten the books on naval warfare."

THE RACE TO DEVELOP NUCLEAR WEAPONS

The United States had entered the atomic age during World War II. In 1939, the noted scientist Albert Einstein wrote to President Franklin D. Roosevelt, warning him that Germany might try to develop an atomic weapon. By 1942, Roosevelt had authorized the U.S. atomic program, known as the Manhattan Project. It was headed by physicist J. Robert Oppenheimer. Another scientist who contributed significantly to the project was physicist Enrico Fermi, who had emigrated to America after fleeing the Fascist regime in Italy.

The power generated by a nuclear reaction occurs when an atom is split in a process known as fission. Simply put, fission occurs when the nucleus of an atom is hit by a neutron from another atom traveling at high speed. The process is similar to what happens when a group of billiard balls is hit with a cue ball. Before the contact, the billiard balls are at rest, tucked together in a tight formation. But when the cue ball hits the formation, the balls explode in all different directions.

When a similar process is performed using atoms instead of billiard balls, a chain reaction commences, causing neutrons to strike the nuclei of other atoms. Since the natural force holding an atom's nucleus together is the most powerful on Earth, the energy released during a fission reaction is tremendous—ten million times stronger than the most powerful coal furnace on Earth. In December 1942, Fermi was able to create a controlled fission reaction in his lab at the University of Chicago. (Fermi had been close to his breakthrough before fleeing Italy. Yet the Fascists under the dictator Benito Mussolini never realized the significance of his work and therefore did not continue his research.)

The American research into developing a nuclear bomb took place in Los Alamos, New Mexico, the headquarters of the Manhattan Project. The Manhattan project was an incredibly complex undertaking, which cost more than $2 billion. It was also kept very secret—hundreds of thousands of people worked on different components of the program, but only a handful knew what the goal of the Manhattan project was. Vice president Harry Truman, for example, was not told about the secret project until after becoming president on the death of Franklin D. Roosevelt in April 1945.

On July 6, 1945, the first atomic bomb was ignited in the desert near Alamogordo, New Mexico. Upon seeing the successful test, Oppenheimer said, "We knew the world would not be the same."

A month after the Trinity test, U.S. warplanes dropped two atomic bombs, nicknamed "Fat Man" and "Little Boy," onto the Japanese cities of Hiroshima and Nagasaki. The two cities were thoroughly devastated by the blasts. Whole neighborhoods were leveled by the explosions. More than 240,000 people died either from the initial explosions or, in the months and years that followed, from cancer and other radioactive-related sicknesses. Faced with such a terrible weapon, the

Italian-born physicist Enrico Fermi (1901–1954) created the first controlled nuclear reaction at the University of Chicago in 1942. His work contributed a great deal to the development of atomic power.

Japanese emperor decided to surrender, ending the Second World War.

The world had never before seen such power or such devastation, but Americans—knowing that the use of the atomic weapons had helped shorten the war and save the lives of American servicemen—endorsed the use of the bombs. A Gallup poll taken in October 1945, just a few months after the Japanese cities were destroyed, posed this question: "Do you wish now that we had never discovered the atomic bomb?" Sixty-two percent of the respondents said no.

The development of nuclear weapons marked the beginning of a new era. The next half-century would be marked by an arms race with the Soviet Union and the development of weapons that could destroy Earth, as well as the harnessing of nuclear energy for peaceful

Regretting the Big Blast

"Do you wish now that we had never discovered the atomic bomb?"

9%
No opinion

29%
Yes

62%
No

Polls taken October 1945; 1,568 total respondents
Source: The Gallup Organization

and commercial purposes, albeit with a heavy price to the environmental health of the world.

FEARS OF NUCLEAR WAR

During the 1950s and early 1960s, most Americans did not know what to make of atomic energy. During the era, the federal government produced a number of educational films advising Americans about how to survive an atomic blast. School children, for example, were told to "duck and cover" — to get under their desks to avoid being struck with debris from the initial blast. Schools ran fallout drills, similar to fire drills, showing children how to find safety in the event of an atomic attack. Schools and other public buildings established fallout shelters in their basements and stocked them with canned food so people could wait out a nuclear attack. Many people did the same in their own basements and backyards. The walls of the shelters were constructed of concrete so they could withstand the blast and act as a barrier against the deadly radioactive fallout that would be carried by the prevailing winds. People bought Geiger counters, sophisticated scientific instruments that measured radioactivity, and kept them in their homes.

In 1961, an average of 5 percent of respondents to Gallup polls said they had made changes to their homes to protect themselves from an atomic bomb attack, while an average of 18 percent of respondents said they had at least stored food to prepare for an atomic attack. A separate Gallup poll in 1961 reported that 22 percent of Americans were "very worried" about "all-out nuclear war," while 37 percent were "fairly worried." Thirty-eight percent, however, were "not at all worried." Wrote pollster George Gallup:

> For most of those families who have taken some steps, it has been a case of storing away food to provide for shortages in the event of a nuclear weapons attack. An estimated 9 million households have done this—

following the suggestion of defense authorities that every family have a two weeks' food supply on hand for this kind of emergency.

An additional 3 million households have gone so far as to make some changes in their home to protect against a nuclear attack—such as reinforcing their cellars, or, in some cases, actually building fallout shelters. About half of these households have also stored food.

Although the majority of U.S. households still have made no such preparation against a nuclear attack, the evidence is that a growing number over the past year have been doing so.

And if people went to the movies in the 1950s, they may have come away with strange ideas about what atomic energy was capable of accomplishing. Among the most popular films of the era were science-fiction movies suggesting that even the most insignificant creatures on Earth could turn into rampaging monsters when exposed to atomic tests. *Them!*, released to theaters in 1954, speculated that a colony of ants could become gigantic simply because the colony was exposed to radioactivity from an atomic test. Other films that told similar stories were *The Deadly Mantis*, *The Beginning of the End*, and *Earth vs. the Spider.*

A family climbs into a backyard fallout shelter, which was designed to survive the blast and radiation from an atomic attack, circa 1955. Such precautions were common during the 1950s and early 1960s, when the prospect of nuclear war seemed imminent.

THE CUBAN MISSILE CRISIS

In 1956, the Central Intelligence Agency commenced a series of flights over the Soviet Union with a jet airplane known as the U-2—an aircraft that could fly at altitudes too high for Soviet radar to detect. The U-2 spy plane made use of high-resolution cameras that could photograph military bases and other top-secret installations on the ground.

By the fall of 1962, U-2 planes were flying over Cuba. This island nation just 90 miles from the Florida coast had fallen under a Communist regime in 1959. The U-2 flights revealed that the Soviet Union had established missile launch sites in Cuba. These missile bases meant the Soviets could launch warheads at Washington, D.C., and other major American cities. On the night of October 22, President John F. Kennedy went on national television to announce the existence of the missile sites and to demand that the Soviets dismantle the sites and withdraw the missiles. Further, Kennedy announced, he had sent the Navy to Cuba to commence a blockade, with orders to turn away any Soviet vessel that approached the island. "It shall be the policy of this nation," he added, "to regard any nuclear missile launched from Cuba against any nation in the Western Hemisphere as an attack by the Soviet

Popular films of the 1950s often depicted ordinary creatures turned into monsters by radioactivity. In this scene from the 1957 movie *The Deadly Mantis*, a gigantic mutant insect demolishes cars and trucks.

Union on the United States, requiring a full retaliatory response upon the Soviet Union."

For four days, the U.S. and the Soviet Union teetered on the brink of nuclear war. Finally, on the evening of October 26, Soviet Premier Nikita Khrushchev said he would withdraw the missiles. (In return, Kennedy secretly agreed to remove U.S. missiles from Turkey, near the border with Russia.) The crisis was over.

THE NUCLEAR ARMS RACE

The world's two superpowers would never again draw so close to nuclear war. However, for most of the next three decades the United States and the Soviet Union pursued a massive arms buildup, each developing thousands of nuclear weapons capable of being fired from submarines or dropped from jet-propelled bombers. In addition, each side developed intercontinental ballistic missiles (ICBMs), which could be launched from underground silos in the home country and sent on flight paths that could quickly cover thousands of miles. Although the two countries occasionally signed treaties limiting the deployment and testing of nuclear weapons, leaders on both sides always suspected that promises would not be kept.

Over the years, Americans reacted to the arms buildup with a growing sense of dread. In 1961, a Gallup poll determined that 43 percent of respondents believed Americans would have a poor chance of surviving a nuclear war. In 1963, the year after the Cuban missile crisis, that belief had increased—52 percent of the people believed they would have a poor chance of surviving a nuclear war. In 1981, after two decades of nuclear arms escalation, the response climbed even further: 60 percent of respondents told a Gallup poll that they would have a poor chance of surviving a nuclear war. What's more, the 1981 poll found that "one American in every five believes the U.S. is 'very likely' to get into an all-our nuclear war in the next 10 years."

Surviving a Nuclear War

"If we should happen to get into an all-out nuclear war, what do you think your own chances would be of living through it — very good, poor, or just 50-50?"

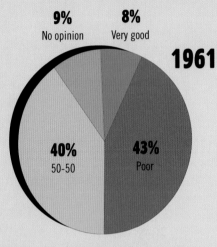

9%
No opinion

8%
Very good

1961

40%
50-50

43%
Poor

Polls taken August 1961; 3,165 total respondents
Source: The Gallup Organization

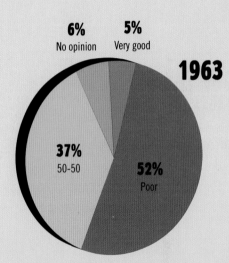

6%
No opinion

5%
Very good

1963

37%
50-50

52%
Poor

Polls taken February 1963; 3,652 total respondents
Source: The Gallup Organization

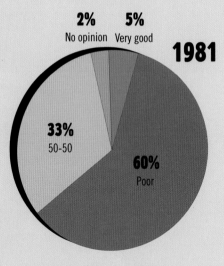

2%
No opinion

5%
Very good

1981

33%
50-50

60%
Poor

Polls taken June 1981; 2,679 total respondents
Source: The Gallup Organization

THE NATIONAL MISSILE DEFENSE SYSTEM

President Ronald Reagan, who took office in January 1981, had a new vision for dealing with the Soviet nuclear threat. He proposed the development of a space-based defense system, the Strategic Defense Initiative (SDI), to protect America from nuclear attack. Nicknamed by critics "Star Wars," after the popular movie that featured a dazzling array of fictional weaponry, the proposed system would employ satellites armed with lasers that could detect and shoot down Soviet missiles before they reached the United States or its allies. In a televised speech to the nation on March 23, 1983, Reagan challenged, "I call upon the scientific community in this country, who gave us nuclear weapons, to turn their great talents to the cause of mankind and world peace; to give us the means of rendering these weapons impotent and obsolete."

Many Americans embraced the concept, even though SDI had a projected cost of as much as one trillion dollars and required the development of new technology. By the mid-1980s, laser beams were employed in

President Ronald Reagan speaks with space shuttle astronauts from the Johnson Space Center in Houston, 1981. During his term as president, Reagan said that space technology should be used to create a national defense against intercontinental ballistic missiles. However, Reagan's proposed Strategic Defense Initiative (derisively nicknamed "Star Wars" by critics) was ultimately abandoned.

many technical capacities—they were built into compact disc players and used to perform intricate surgeries, for example—but the use of the highly concentrated light beams to shoot down an ICBM was—and still is—the stuff of science fiction.

Still, Gallup polls taken during 1985 found approximately four in ten Americans in support, in general, of the Star Wars missile defense system. Some of them told pollsters that the development of SDI would possibly reduce the chance of war or increase the chance of a nuclear arms agreement. This impression proved on target, for the specter of laser-armed satellites orbiting the Earth did, in fact, provoke Soviet leaders to propose reductions in nuclear arms. That year, Soviet Premier Mikhail Gorbachev proposed a bilateral reduction in arms, cutting the weapons forces of the two nations by half, if Reagan agreed to scuttle the Strategic Defense Initiative. Americans were suspicious about Gorbachev's promise, however. Wrote pollster George Gallup Jr., "Lack of trust has been the basic reason Americans have been wary of entering into any bilateral or unilateral disarmament treaties with the Soviet Union. If assured of verification, the vast majority of U.S. citizens would support such treaties."

The situation was drastically altered in 1991 when the Soviet Union collapsed, bringing a sudden end to the Cold War that had dominated life in both hemispheres for some four decades. Still, while the Soviet threat disintegrated, other threats have surfaced, and nuclear weapons remain a reality of modern society. Russia, which emerged as the dominant nuclear power in the East following the breakup of the Soviet Union, has signed an arms limitation agreement with the United States, yet other nations with nuclear capabilities, or suspected of having such capabilities, that have not taken such steps may pose a greater danger. Today, U.S. leaders feel the greatest potential threat is from "rogue nations" like North Korea or

Iran, which have either developed, or are actively trying to develop, nuclear weapons. In addition, both India and Pakistan now possess nuclear weapons; the neighboring countries have fought several wars since 1947, and some experts feel their next conflict will involve a nuclear exchange.

Although the Strategic Defense Initiative was scrapped following the breakup of the Soviet Union, in 1999 Congress authorized development of a National Missile Defense System, which would employ sophisticated radar and ground-based rockets to intercept incoming missiles. In 2000, a Gallup poll found 55 percent of Americans supporting this development, although in tests to date the system has been a failure.

PEACEFUL USES OF NUCLEAR POWER

Nuclear fission does not only cause horrific destruction; it can also be controlled and harnessed as a source of energy. On June 28, 1955, an experimental nuclear power reactor known as BORAX went on line, providing energy to the city of Arco, Idaho. BORAX—which stood for Boiling Reactor Experiment—used a nuclear reaction to boil water and create steam, which then powered turbines to produce electricity. The reactor was developed by the University of Chicago and the federal government's Argonne National Laboratory. Two years later, the first commercially developed nuclear power plant went on line, providing electricity to the city of Santa Susana, California. Many other major power companies soon followed suit. Throughout the 1960s, they erected nuclear plants to provide electricity to America's largest cities.

Americans were quick to embrace nuclear energy as a source of everyday power. A Gallup poll in 1956 found 67 percent of respondents believing that American industry would, in some way, adopt the use of atomic energy within ten years. Further, 70 percent of

Americans said they would feel safe sharing their community with an atomic power plant.

ENVIRONMENTAL CONCERNS

That attitude would change, however, as concerns about the safety of the plants and their effects on the environment surfaced. Over the years, mishaps occurred at some plants, causing radioactive gases to leak into the air. Concerns were also raised about the safety of storing spent radioactive fuel, which remains highly volatile for years after it is taken out of use. By 1976, Americans were not as sure that atomic energy was safe: that year a Gallup poll found just 34 percent of Americans believing that safety regulations at nuclear power plants were sufficient. "Nearly half (45 percent) of the survey respondents say they would object to having a nuclear plant constructed near their home (within a radius of five miles)," Gallup reported.

Three years later, the United States suffered its most serious nuclear plant accident when a series of design errors, mechanical failures, and human miscalculations led to the partial meltdown of the nuclear core in Unit 2 of the Three Mile Island power plant near Harrisburg, Pennsylvania. The accident occurred when the fissionable uranium at the reactor core was left uncovered by water, allowing the core to heat to some 4,000° Fahrenheit and start melting. At such temperatures, nothing could have stopped the core from melting through the floor of the reactor, right into the ground below — spreading nuclear contamination into the environment and possibly causing a tremendous explosion.

Fortunately, at Three Mile Island, the core was cooled before undergoing a complete meltdown; nevertheless, during the accident radioactive gases were vented into the air. Although evacuations were not ordered, some 135,000 local residents — about 20 percent of those living within a twenty-mile radius of the plant — chose to leave their homes.

Following the accident, 60 percent of respondents told Gallup pollsters they would object if a nuclear plant were constructed within five miles of their homes. Just 23 percent of the respondents felt safety regulations at nuclear plants were adequate.

Seven years after the Three Mile Island accident, a nuclear plant located near the city of Chernobyl in the Ukraine (at the time, part of the Soviet Union) suffered an even more devastating accident when an explosion and fire in the plant's reactor core released radioactive gases. These gases spread throughout the Soviet Union and eastern European countrysides, killing at least thirty-one people and infecting possibly thousands more with long-term, and possibly life-threatening, illnesses such as cancer. A Gallup poll taken shortly after the Chernobyl accident found 65 percent of Americans favoring stricter safety measures for nuclear power plants.

Aside from concerning themselves with safety considerations, those investing in nuclear plants had to worry about costs. The cost of building nuclear plants had become prohibitive—it was not unusual for power companies to invest a billion dollars or more in construction of the facilities. Pollster George Gallup Jr. summed up what he regarded as a limited future for nuclear power plants in the United States:

> Although the Chernobyl explosion undoubtedly revived Americans' fears about the danger of nuclear plants, the future of nuclear power in the U.S. was already in doubt. . . .
>
> Currently, 100 plants are operating in the U.S., generating about 16% of the nation's electricity. When the 27 plants now under construction are completed, nuclear energy will account for about 20% of total capacity.
>
> Aside from the political issues involved, economic factors may rule out future construction of U.S. nuclear generators. Although the uranium fuel used has remained cheap, the cost of building and operating these

This satellite photograph shows the area around the Chernobyl nuclear power plant in the Soviet Union, shortly after a deadly reactor accident in April 1986. The red areas of the photograph are tainted by high radioactivity.

plants has soared, compared with the cost of coal-fired plants. Thus additional nuclear plants may be unable to compete with other energy sources solely on the basis of economics.

Today, there are more than 430 commercial nuclear power plants operating throughout the world. More than 100 of these are located in the United States, where they provide about 20 percent of the nation's total electric energy power. That percentage may actually increase in the next few decades, depending on the price of oil. Increases in oil prices during 2004 and 2005 made it more expensive for power plants to use that fuel to generate electricity. While nuclear power does provide an inexpensive source of energy, U.S. leaders will have to balance the benefits of atomic energy with the potential environmental and health hazards.

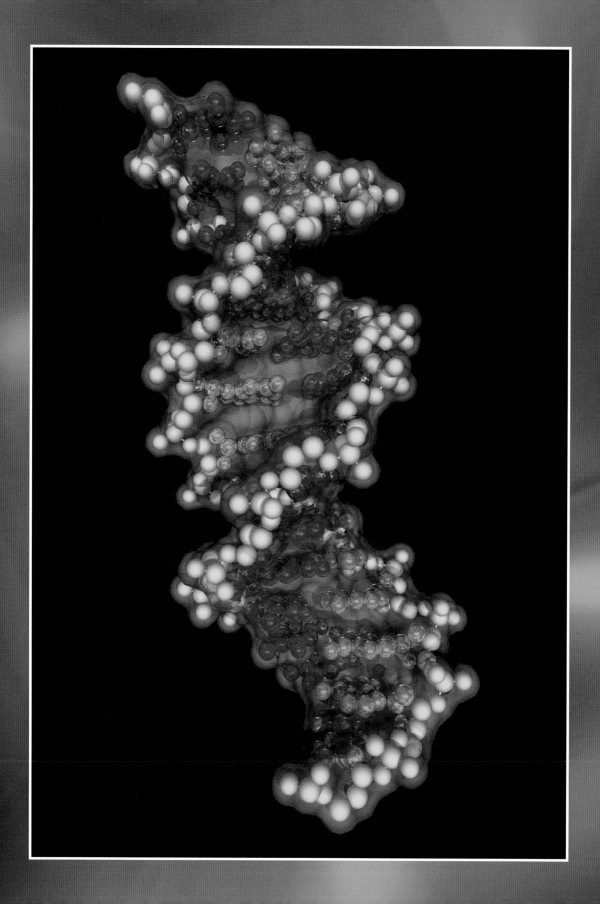

TINKERING WITH DNA

In the spring of 1953, a Gallup poll posed what was then a rather startling question to 1,602 Americans: "Do you think that science will ever be able to create life?" Seventy-eight percent of the respondents didn't think so, but 9 percent thought it would be possible to create some form of life in a test tube.

The notion that life could be created in the laboratory would turn out to be far more plausible than it may have sounded in 1953. In fact, just a few weeks after the Gallup poll was taken, two British scientists announced the discovery that every cell in every living thing on Earth contains deoxyribonucleic acid (DNA). The two scientists, James Dewey Watson and Francis Crick, said DNA takes the shape of the "double helix"—a twisted ladder—and that each rung of the ladder holds a different characteristic of genetic code. This means that different parts of the DNA molecule spell out, for example, whether a person has brown or blue eyes or dark or blond hair, whether that person is tall or short, or whether that person leads a disease-free life or is saddled with ailments passed

The computer simulation on the opposite page shows the double helix structure of DNA. Since the discovery of DNA by Watson and Crick, scientists have sought greater understanding of how DNA determines the physical characteristics of living things.

down from previous generations, such as Alzheimer's disease or Parkinson's disease. Likewise, insects, trees, monkeys, bumblebees, violets, zebras, and every other plant and animal on the planet owe its characteristics to the makeup of its own particular strand of DNA.

Watson and Crick could not tell which rung of the ladder controlled hair color and which controlled eye color, but they speculated that if researchers could ever unravel the mysteries of the genetic code, then it might be possible to duplicate the code in a laboratory — to "clone" a living thing — creating an exact duplicate of the specimen that donated the DNA to the process. Watson and Crick wrote in the scientific journal *Nature*, "It has not escaped our notice that the specific pairing we have postulated immediately suggests a possible copying mechanism for the genetic material."

Watson and Crick won the Nobel Prize for their work. Their discovery of DNA's role in the development of plants, humans, and other animals was one of the most significant scientific advancements of the 20th century. One of the best-known applications of DNA technology has been in law enforcement; criminals who leave smears of blood or even loose hair from their heads at the scene of a crime have been identified through DNA analysis. Conversely, many defendants on trial or wrongly convicted of a crime have been exonerated after a DNA analysis showed they could not possibly have been involved in the offense.

Physicians have also been able to take DNA samples from a fetus in its mother's womb and tell whether there is a strong possibility the baby will be born with a disease that is transmitted genetically. The most common disease uncovered in this test is Down's syndrome; symptoms of this condition include severe mental retardation as well as limited development of many physical abilities.

Further genetic advances took place in 2001, when researchers unveiled a map of the human genetic

James Watson and Francis Crick (both pictured in 1993) discovered that DNA is the basic unit of all life on Earth. Their work, which earned them the 1962 Nobel Prize, has led to great scientific advancement in the late twentieth century.

code—identifying some forty thousand genes that make up a person. What was most startling about the composition of the map was that it was not terribly more complicated than the map of a common worm, which is composed of some eighteen thousand genes. "If we were banking on our human pride being derived from the number of genes we have, it was a pretty black day when the numbers came forward," said Dr. Francis Collins, director of the National Human Genome Research Institute.

But there have been setbacks in genetic research as well. For instance, in 1999 18-year-old Jesse Gelsinger agreed to take part in an experimental therapy at the University of Pennsylvania in Philadelphia, in hopes of finding a cure for his rare liver disorder. Gelsinger's body would be injected with healthy genetic material, but the genes had to be delivered in viruses. Over the years, researchers had found that the body's immune system would defeat such viruses, wiping them out as well as the therapeutic DNA. To combat this problem, scientists at the University of Pennsylvania tried to thwart the immune system by injecting Gelsinger with heavy doses of viruses. In a PBS documentary titled *Gene Therapy*, Jesse's father, Paul Gelsinger, explained his son's situation: "He believed, after discussions with representatives from Penn, that the worst that could happen in the trial would be that he would have flu-like symptoms for a week. He was excited to help."

Instead of experiencing flu-like symptoms, however, Jesse Gelsinger went into shock and then a coma. Finally, the teenager died from the bombardment of viruses. Medical researchers believe that Gelsinger's death had set back gene therapy by years. Joseph Glorioso, president of the American Society of Gene Therapy, remarked, "It was really a surprise and a disappointment, and it caused the medical and scientific community to launch an all-out effort to understand the basis of this event and to begin to think about ways to circumvent the problem."

DOLLY THE SHEEP

Still, genetic researchers maintain that manipulation of DNA holds great promise for curing disease. Through the process known as "therapeutic cloning," for example, so-called stem cells can be grown by using a donor's DNA. The stem cells are then used to replace diseased or damaged cells in a sick person's body.

Therapeutic cloning has found many opponents, among them people who believe cloning of stem cells can lead to cloning of humans. In recent years, several Gallup polls have asked Americans whether they favor cloning cells in order to create a human being. Invariably, a majority of the respondents oppose this.

Despite the claims of some scientists with dubious credentials, to date no one has succeeded in cloning a

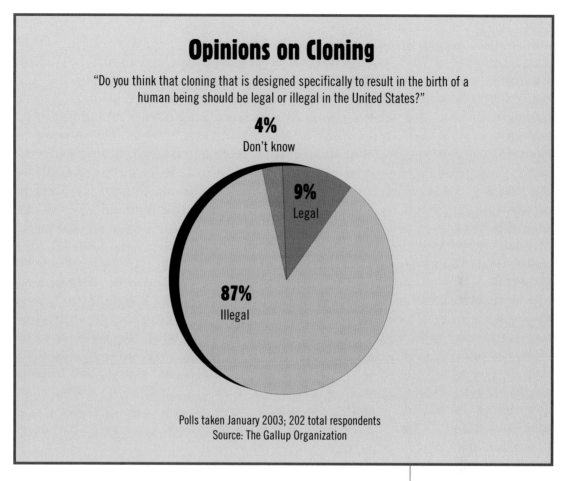

Opinions on Cloning

"Do you think that cloning that is designed specifically to result in the birth of a human being should be legal or illegal in the United States?"

4%
Don't know

9%
Legal

87%
Illegal

Polls taken January 2003; 202 total respondents
Source: The Gallup Organization

human embryo. To prevent this from occurring, many state legislatures in the United States have enacted prohibitions against human cloning. In 1997, President Bill Clinton banned the use of federal funds for human cloning experiments. "Each human life is unique, born of a miracle that reaches beyond laboratory science," Clinton said when he announced the ban. "I believe we must respect this profound gift and resist the temptation to replicate ourselves."

Cloning is accomplished when a scientist withdraws the nucleus from a cell and transplants it into another cell that lacks a nucleus. In 1972, a tadpole was cloned by Oxford University biologist John Gurdon, who transplanted the nucleus from a cell of a frog into an unfertilized egg of another frog; that egg's nucleus had been destroyed by an ultraviolet light. The manipulated egg grew into a tadpole that was a clone of the frog which had donated the nucleus. To look at this another way, the tadpole was born without the consummation of a sexual union between the father and mother. The mother frog's egg had not been fertilized.

The process sounds similar to in vitro fertilization, but there are important differences. In vitro fertilization was developed in 1978 to assist women who experience difficulty conceiving a child. Using this process, when a woman is unable to conceive, physicians withdraw an egg from the woman's ovary and unite it in the laboratory with a cell from her husband's sperm. After the egg is fertilized, it becomes an embryo and is placed in the woman's womb. In the womb, it will grow into a fetus and, in nine months, it will be born. While there is no sexual union involved in the conception of the fetus, the mother's normal egg is fertilized with a cell from the father. Therefore, the embryo includes DNA from both parents—just as any child would. This stands in contrast to cloning, which involves no melding of DNA. Only the donor's DNA remains in the egg; therefore, the embryo is not an offspring of the parents, but rather a "twin" of the donor.

Gurdon's tadpole died soon after its birth, but research continued. In 1997, Scottish geneticist Ian Wilmut at the Roslin Institute in Edinburgh announced to a stunned world that he had cloned a sheep named Dolly. Wilmut had used techniques pioneered by Gurdon, but with many revisions. For example, to prompt the egg to accept the donor nucleus, Wilmut used a gentle pulse of electricity. He attempted the technique 277 times. In all those attempts, just twenty-nine eggs accepted the donor nuclei. These eggs became embryos, but twenty-eight of the twenty-nine embryos died before birth. Only Dolly survived. She was a clone of her "twin" sister, who happened to be six years older.

OPPOSITION TO CLONING

Once the news about Dolly was reported, opponents of cloning started lining up with some very loud and clear concerns. Chief among them was the fear that if a sheep could be cloned, so could a human. Opponents believed that the creation of life should be a sacred process involving a commitment between a man and woman to conceive. They argued that a child deserves the opportunity to grow into a person whose path in life is not predetermined by a genetic plan worked out ahead of time. Critics argued that if cloning humans was permitted to proceed, parents could search for a donor with specific characteristics. Why not find a donor with the looks of a movie star or the athleticism of a quarterback? Through cloning, they claimed, a

Dr. Ian Wilmut sits with Dolly, the cloned sheep, in March 1996. Since his successful cloning experiment, Wilmut has spoken against "irresponsible" attempts to clone humans.

BIOENGINEERED FOODS

Scientists have been able to alter the DNA of plants, enabling farmers to grow crops that are hardier in bad weather conditions and more resistant to insects and diseases. But tinkering with DNA for the purpose of producing better crops has also sparked a national debate. Many people oppose bioengineered food, believing it is unsafe.

One such example involves papaya. In 1998, papaya farmers in Hawaii found their crops infested with Papaya Ring Spot Virus, or PRSV, which is spread by insects. Their plight came to the attention of agronomists at Cornell University in New York, who were able to isolate the gene that caused the virus. Next, they injected the gene-carrying virus into a papaya plant, providing it with an immunization against the virus spread by the insects. Soon, Hawaiian papayas were immunized against PRSV.

While it would seem that manipulating DNA saved the papaya crop from PRSV, many people wonder what else the genetic change may have done to the plant. They fear that the changes could have made the papayas dangerous to eat—a fact that might not become evident for years. Opponents of bioengineered food are particularly worried that people with food allergies might undergo an unexpected reaction if they consume bioengineered foods.

"The Food and Drug Administration is confident that the genetically engineered food products on the U.S. market today are as safe as their conventionally bred counterparts, and the agency is prepared to meet the safety and regulatory challenges presented by new products as they emerge from the laboratory," Mark B. McClellan, head of the FDA, told the magazine *FDA Consumer* for its November 1, 2003, issue. "Genetically engineered foods must adhere to the same high standards of safety under the Federal Food, Drug and Cosmetic Act that apply to more traditional food products."

Over the years, Gallup polls have indicated that most Americans are not afraid to eat bioengineered foods. In 2003, just 34 percent of respondents thought bioengineered foods represented a health hazard, while 54 percent thought the foods were safe to eat. The Gallup analysis stated, "Biotechnology has a great deal of potential, and currently enjoys a relatively high level of support among Americans. However, this support places great responsibility on the Food and Drug Administration, the U.S. Department of Agriculture and the Environmental Protection Agency to ensure that benefits are achieved without exposing the U.S. population to significant risks."

parent could virtually guarantee that a child would grow up looking like Brad Pitt or with the ability to throw a football like Brett Favre does. Boston College bioethics professor John Paris told *Time* magazine, "Choosing personal characteristics as if they were options on a car is an invitation to misadventure. It is in the diversity of our population that we find interest and enthusiasm."

Other critics pointed out that cloning a human to become a great singer, author, or athlete is no guarantee of success. After all, many famous and talented people also suffer from mental illness, alcoholism, and drug abuse. Rabbi Moshe Tendler, professor of biology and biblical law at Yeshiva University in New York, told *Time*, "I can make myself an Albert Einstein, and he may turn out to be a drug addict."

Wilmut himself emerged as a major opponent of human cloning. He explained that he had cloned Dolly not to take a step toward the cloning of a human, but to take a step toward creating a better species of sheep whose wool would be much more desirable. Following the birth of Dolly, other geneticists experimented with Wilmut's techniques. They have not been able to improve much on Wilmut's results—the failure rate of cloned animals is believed to be 98 percent. As for the cloned animals that made it to birth, many have been born with birth defects—their organs have been too large or they have been born with poor immune systems. Wilmut has warned that if scientists attempt to clone humans, there is a strong possibility that many human babies could be born with similar defects. The risks are so great that he has declared it "criminally irresponsible" for scientists to experiment with human cloning. Following the birth of Dolly, Wilmut told *Time* magazine, "We had a cloned sheep born . . . that was clearly not normal. We hoped for a few days it would improve and then, out of kindness, we euthanized it, because it obviously would never be healthy."

Further objection to human cloning comes from people who harbor deeply religious beliefs. They argue that God implants the human soul in the child at the moment of conception. They argue that discarding hundreds of human embryos through the cloning process is akin to mass murder. "Each of the embryos is a human being simply by dint of its genetic make-up," said David Byers, director of the National Conference of Catholic Bishops's Commission on Science and Human Values.

MORALLY AMBIGUOUS LINE

But there is another side to the issue of genetics that has garnered widespread support from many medical researchers. In recent years, debate has raged over the value of embryonic stem cell research. Embryonic stem cells are believed to hold the secrets to cure some of society's most horrific diseases—juvenile diabetes, Alzheimer's disease, and Parkinson's disease among them. Stem cells might also help with other physical problems. Before he died in late 2004, the actor Christopher Reeve, who had been paralyzed in a 1995 horseback-riding accident, made an appeal for stem cell research, arguing that it could be employed to cure debilitating spinal injuries.

When transplanted into a person's body, stem cells are believed to be able to replicate and replace damaged or diseased cells. But the stem cells must come from embryos that are only a few days old, and virtually the only viable source for the cells are embryos created and frozen at in vitro fertilization clinics. Those who believe life begins at conception consider stem cell research morally wrong because it removes cells from the birth process and does not give them the chance to develop into babies. In 2004, a Gallup poll found that 57 percent of British respondents found stem cell research morally acceptable, while the same poll found 54 percent of Americans believing it morally acceptable. The poll

also found 61 percent of Canadians supporting stem cell research.

Another source of stem cells could be through reproducing them in the process known as therapeutic cloning, essentially the same process that led to the birth of Dolly the sheep. Michael West, president of a Massachusetts biotech company that hopes to use cloning technology to develop human medicines, told *Time* magazine, "What we're doing is the first step toward cloning a human being, but we're not cloning a human being. The miracle of cloning isn't what people think it is. Cloning allows you to make a genetically identical copy of an animal, yes, but in the eyes of a biologist, the real miracle is seeing a skin cell being put

Actor Christopher Reeve, Senator Ted Kennedy of Massachusetts, and Senator Dianne Feinstein of California discuss their support of therapeutic cloning at a press conference. After an accident left him paralyzed, Reeve became an advocate for stem cell research.

Opinions on Stem Cell Research

"Do you personally believe that in general it is morally acceptable or morally wrong to conduct medical research using stem cells obtained from human embryos?"

3%
Depends on the situation

6%
Don't know/refused

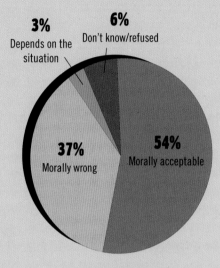

37%
Morally wrong

54%
Morally acceptable

2004 Opinions

Polls taken May 2004; 1,000 total respondents
Source: The Gallup Organization

2%
Depends on the situation

7%
Don't know/refused

2002 Opinions

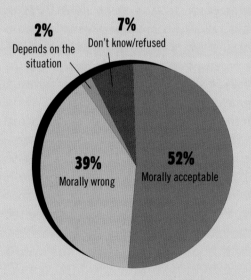

39%
Morally wrong

52%
Morally acceptable

Polls taken May 2002; 1,012 total respondents
Source: The Gallup Organization

back into the egg cell, taking it back in time to when it was an undifferentiated cell, which then can turn into any cell in the body."

Some states as well as foreign countries that have outlawed human cloning have since relaxed their regulations to permit therapeutic cloning. In 2000, for example, Great Britain relaxed its laws to permit therapeutic cloning. In the United States, a 2002 Gallup poll found that 34 percent of respondents found it acceptable to clone human embryos for use in medical research. In the same poll, 52 percent of respondents said they found it "morally acceptable" to employ embryonic stem cells harvested from in vitro fertilization clinics in medical research.

For now, scientists look at the potential of stem cell research and therapeutic cloning and wonder whether the value of the science makes it acceptable to cross a morally ambiguous line. Leon Kass, a professor of social thought at the University of Chicago, told *Time* magazine, "Science is close to crossing some horrendous boundaries. Here is an opportunity for human beings to decide if we're simply going to stand in the path of the technological steamroller or take control and help guide its direction."

7

MAKING LIVES BETTER: THE COMPUTER AND THE INTERNET

By the time the U.S. Census Bureau completed the 1880 census, it was clear that the next census, scheduled to begin in 1890, would pose considerable problems. Because Census Bureau workers had to tabulate all the numbers by hand, the 1880 census had taken seven years to complete. The documents the agency produced, all based on statistical analyses of how the population of the United States had grown, were written after the bureau's analysts had performed all the mathematical computations by hand.

Officials knew the speed of the census-taking process had to be improved, not only because it had been so tedious and time-consuming, but because between 1880 and 1890, the population of the United States was expected to grow by approximately 20 percent. As the start of the

The Hollerith tabulator (opposite) greatly simplified the process of compiling census data. It took seven years for analysts to tabulate results of the 1880 census; using Hollerith's machine, tabulation of the 1890 census data was completed in six weeks.

1890 census approached, officials at the Census Bureau feared that the counting and analysis of the numbers would not be completed until after 1900 — the date when the next census was scheduled to begin. And so the Census Bureau made a plea to American inventors for a device that could tabulate data automatically. Census Bureau workers would still count people directly — in most cases, knocking on their doors to ask questions about the size of their households — but the agency needed a device that could take the data they gathered, record it, and then make the information available to the organization's analysts.

In many ways, that last function would be the most important. Perhaps one analyst would need to know how many women under the age of 40 lived in a specific part of the United States. Another analyst might need to know how many children attended school in a particular city. The government uses such information when deciding how to spend money for social programs. Under the system used for the 1880 census, each analyst had to go to the original documents prepared by the census takers and derive the specific information he or she needed. It was a long and cumbersome process, which is why it had taken seven years to tabulate the data from the 1880 census.

As it turned out, the Census Bureau did not have to search too far to find a solution to its problem. In 1882, Massachusetts Institute of Technology engineering professor Herman Hollerith started work on a device he called the Hollerith Electric Tabulating System. In 1894, Hollerith left MIT for a job in Washington, D.C., at the U.S. Patents Office. While working in Washington, Hollerith learned of the Census Bureau's problem and offered it his tabulating machine.

The machine was partially based on a device used for weaving fabric, known as the Jacquard Loom. The loom's inventor, Frenchman Joseph-Maire Jacquard, realized that weaving was a rather tedious and repetitive process, and so he developed a mechanical loom that operated by using stiff cards perforated with holes. As the loom moved, the holes in the cards determined which color thread would slip through to form the patterns in the fabric.

Hollerith applied the same principle to his tabulating system. When his machine was used for the census, every person in the United States was assigned a "punch card" that had been perforated with holes, with each hole located in a certain spot to represent a different fact about the citizen. The holes were punched in ways to reflect gender, age, marital status, number of children, and other factors. As each card was fed into the tabulator, the holes lined up with pins that would complete an electrical circuit. The current activated a mechanical counter, which kept track of the numbers. Of course, in places where there were no holes, the pins would not meet and the counter remained idle.

The Census Bureau employed the Hollerith Electric Tabulating System for the 1890 census. Once Hollerith's invention was put to use the census numbers were tabulated in six weeks.

Hollerith soon received a patent for his tabulator and founded his own business, the Tabulating Machine Company. The name of the company was later changed to the Computer Tabulating Recording Company. Hollerith retired in 1921, but the company carried on. Three years after the founder's retirement, the company changed its name again, this time to International Business Machines, or IBM. Today IBM is one of the largest manufacturers of computer technology in the world.

ORIGINS OF THE COMPUTER

It would be wrong to suggest that Herman Hollerith invented the computer. Hollerith made an early contribution to the technology that would lead to the computer—punch cards, for example, remained a method of recording data for use by computers well into the early 1980s. Still, the history of the computer can be seen as starting much earlier than Hollerith's work, if one defines the word "computer" more broadly. It could be argued, for instance, that human beings have searched for computing devices to save them the labor of calculating and recording data as far back as 1300 B.C., when the Chinese first used the abacus.

During the ensuing centuries, many inventors and tinkerers developed mechanical devices that could make simple—and even not so simple—mathematical computations. These devices usually employed levers, wheels, gears, springs, and other parts commonly found in clocks. In 1623 a German inventor named Wilhelm Schickard developed what he called the "Calculating Clock," which could add and subtract six-digit numbers. When a user asked the clock to compute a number that was too large for its gears to handle, a bell went off.

The drive to develop a machine that could calculate numbers and perform other functions quickly and accurately continued into the twentieth century. In 1935, IBM developed the IBM 601. By reading data from punch cards, the 601 could perform a multiplication problem in one second. During World War II, researchers at Harvard University developed the Harvard Mark I, which processed data by using vacuum tubes. The Mark I was 50 feet long and weighed five tons. It could add and subtract in three-tenths of a second, but division took twelve seconds. The head of the Mark I project, Howard Aiken, believed it took so long to calculate numbers because the computer had too many gears, levers, and other moving parts.

Aiken moved from the Mark I to an even more ambitious wartime project, development of the Electronic Numerical Integrator and Computer, or ENIAC. ENIAC was built and designed at the University of Pennsylvania to calculate the ranges of large cannons—information gunners could use when aiming the weapons. The war ended before ENIAC was completed, but the computer's ability to calculate complex equations set a new standard in computer technology. ENIAC could perform 100,000 calculations a second. It also weighed 30 tons and employed some 18,000 vacuum tubes, requiring so much electricity that when ENIAC ran at its peak it was said to have dimmed lights throughout Philadelphia. And although ENIAC could solve problems in a fraction of a second, it might take days to enter the problem in the first place. Engineers had to manage ENIAC's mass of cables and switches that had to be repositioned and reset for each calculation. And there was, of course, no computer screen to display the answer in neat, electronically generated characters. Data went into ENIAC on punch cards and came out on punch cards.

Nevertheless, ENIAC is widely regarded as the first successful electronic computer. Following the war, research and development on the technology continued to be funded by large corporations. New innovations were added. For example, it was found that data could be stored on magnetic tape rather than punch cards. In 1948, innovators found a way to adopt a teletype machine to a computer, thereby making it possible for the computer to provide its data on a typewritten page. Some engineers even tried various ways to make computers smaller and to eliminate a lot of their moving parts. In 1949, *Popular Mechanics* magazine predicted, "Computers in the future may weigh no more than 1.5 tons." Despite that note of optimism, computers were still big and noisy.

American corporations found many uses for computers. The machines stored and retrieved data on employees and customers. They were useful for bookkeeping. Credit card companies, which were becoming popular during the 1950s, relied heavily on computers to keep track of people's accounts. In 1951, the U.S.

Census Bureau took delivery of the UNIVAC I computer, which it used to help analyze the data generated by the 1950 census. At the time, no one could envision the impact computers would have on people's lives by the end of the century.

THE PERSONAL COMPUTER

In the 1950s, few Americans knew much about computers or understood what they could do. In 1957, a Gallup poll asked people to name a company in the computer business; 61 percent of the respondents could not provide an answer. Also in 1957, the head of the business books division for publisher Prentice Hall uttered this now-famous statement: "I have traveled the length and breadth of this country and talked with the best people, and I can assure you that data processing is a fad that won't last the year."

Two men program the enormous UNIVAC computer, circa 1959.

Although computers shrank in the 1950s, they still took up entire rooms. But in 1958, innovators adapted integrated circuits to computers, using tiny electronic circuits to replace the moving parts and vacuum tubes. A decade later, the microchip was developed. With that, circuitry could be implanted into a tiny silicon chip, making it possible to build a computer small enough to fit on a desk. By the early 1970s, screens and keyboards were adopted for computer use as well.

In 1972, computer engineer Nolan Bushnell developed the first game that could be played on a computer. He called it Pong, and it was essentially a game of virtual table tennis. Two rackets were controlled by competing players, who smacked a little white dot back and forth until someone missed. Knobs on a console controlled the rackets; the push of a button served the ball. Bushnell first tried to sell the game to a computer company, but when he was turned down he started his own company, which he named Atari. In November 1972, the first Pong game was installed in a bar named Andy Capp's in San Jose, California. Within days, the place was packed with players eager to drop quarters into the machine's slot. The video game boom was born.

Soon, the San Jose area became the computer technology capital of the United States. Nicknamed "Silicon Valley," the region attracted young people full of ideas about developing computers, peripherals, and software. Many of them attended nearby Stanford University, which was admitting the best and brightest. Two young people working in this climate were Steve Jobs, who had a job designing games for Atari, and Steve Wozniak, who worked for Hewlett-Packard, which manufactured electronic calculators.

At this point, small computers had been introduced on the market, but they were expensive and complicated and the market for them was essentially limited to hobbyists and engineers. Most home computers were sold as kits, which meant the purchaser had to assemble the parts. "All the little computer kits that were being touted to hobbyists in 1975 were square or rectangular boxes with non-understandable switches on them," Wozniak recalled.

In 1976, Wozniak designed and built his own personal computer. It was cobbled together from assorted electronic parts, all fastened to a plank of plywood, but on March 1 of that year he showed it off to the members of a computer club on the Stanford campus. Their reception to Wozniak's machine was overwhelming. Prior to the meeting, it had never occurred to Wozniak that if he had brought multiple computers to the club, he could sell them all. But the marketability of Wozniak's computer occurred to his friend Jobs, who immediately suggested that a small, inexpensive personal computer could sell—and not just to hobbyists. "Steve didn't do one circuit, design, or piece of code," said Wozniak. "But it never crossed my mind to sell computers. It was Steve who said, 'Let's hold them up in the air and sell a few.'"

At first, the two men pitched the idea of the personal computer to their employers. But when neither Hewlett-Packard nor Atari showed interest, Jobs and Wozniak formed their own company—they named it Apple because Jobs had a part-time job at an apple orchard—and produced their first computer, the Apple I. To raise the $1,750 they needed to buy circuit boards, Wozniak sold his calculator while Jobs found a buyer for his old Volkswagen bus. The company was officially formed on April 1, 1976—one month after Wozniak's demonstration in front of the computer club at Stanford.

Wozniak and Jobs intended to sell the computers as kits, but when a retailer promised to buy 500 of the machines as long as they were assembled, Jobs, Wozniak, and some friends hunkered down in Jobs' garage, where they worked furiously to assemble the computers. Finally, Apple delivered its first 500 computers, and the company made a profit of $8,000. Soon, Apple grew into one of the largest computer companies on the planet.

Other young entrepreneurs interested in computers were developing their own ideas. For example, college students Paul Allen and Bill Gates formed a company they called Traf-O-Data, which made car counters for highway departments. In 1975, Allen and Gates changed the name of the company to Microsoft and also changed the company's focus to designing software for computers. In 1974, Traf-O-Data had earned Allen and Gates a profit of a mere $252. Yet within a decade, the success of Microsoft would make both men billionaires.

DEVELOPMENT OF THE INTERNET

There was one final significant development in the story of computers during this era. In 1969, the Advanced Research Projects Agency Network (ARPANET), was created by the U.S. Department of Defense as a way for military computers to share information. It had long been easy enough for computers to swap data—floppy disks had been around since 1950—but by using ARPANET, computers could be connected over telephone lines.

The Department of Defense enlisted the Stanford Research Institute in California to design ARPANET. On October 29, 1969, at 10:30 P.M., a computer at the University of California at Los Angeles communicated with a computer at Stanford, approximately 370 miles away. The first message was transmitted by UCLA

Apple cofounder Steve Jobs was among the first people to understand that there would be a market for personal computers. Today, Apple remains on the cutting edge of digital technology.

engineering professor Leonard Kleinrock, assisted by his student Charley Kline. The message was supposed to be the word "login," but the system crashed before the full word could be typed. Because of the crash, the first word transmitted over ARPANET was "lo." An hour later, the system was rebooted and the full message was sent.

ARPANET grew slowly. By 1977, there were 111 computers on the network. In 1984, 1,000 computers were being served. By then, though, ARPANET was opened to nonmilitary users, including large corporations and universities. As a result, it didn't take long for ARPANET use to explode. In 1990, ARPANET was officially dissolved. It had evolved into what is known today as the Internet.

SUBSTANTIAL IMPACT ON PEOPLE'S LIVES

Since the days when Jobs and Wozniak tinkered in a garage and Gates and Allen wrote the code for what would become the first Microsoft operating systems, computers have become cheaper, smaller, and easier to use. They have also become essential to people's lives. Over the years, Gallup polls have found that people have come to rely more and more on computers and the Internet. In 1987, just 16 percent of respondents to a Gallup poll said they used a computer at home, while 33 percent said they used a computer at work. By 2003, however, 83 percent of respondents to a Gallup poll said they used computers either at home or at work.

As for the Internet, Americans have found hundreds of uses. A 2004 Gallup poll found that at least 45 percent of American adults use the Internet every day. People between the ages of 18 and 29 use the Internet most frequently, according to the poll, which found that 55 percent of the people in that age range use the Internet every day. As age increases, daily Internet usage decreases. Forty-four percent of people between the ages of 50 and 64 use the Internet daily, while just 17 percent of people over the age of 65 use the Internet daily. Gallup reported: "Regular Internet access has become the norm for an increasingly broad spectrum of people, though older Americans tend to use it less heavily. And the youngest Americans are virtually guaranteed to become familiarized with the Web. According to the National Center for Education Statistics, by the beginning of the school year in 2001, 99% of all U.S. public schools had access to the Internet, up from 35% in 1994."

The numbers from the 2004 Gallup poll reflect only those Americans who use the Internet daily. Certainly, others may not have a reason to log on every day, but for them the Internet still may be an important part of their lives. A 2005 Gallup poll found that 76 percent of Americans use the Internet either at home, work, or school. That number increased by 8 percent over what had been recorded in a similar poll in 2002.

The 2004 Gallup poll found that 65 percent of all adults use the Internet to send e-mail, 41 percent use the Web to check the news and weather, and 21 percent send instant messages over the Internet. In addition, the poll said 20 percent of adults use the Net to pay their bills, 18 percent make travel plans on-line, 16 percent play on-line games, 16 percent rely on the Internet to help them plan their personal finances, 15 percent shop over the Internet, and 12 percent use it to seek medical advice. In conducting the poll, Gallup researchers interviewed a number of Internet users. The interviews were conducted over the Internet, using instant messaging.

In a June 2001 Gallup Poll of 341 email users, 96 percent said they believed that the Internet had "made their lives better."

The Internet may have become an important part of people's lives, but there is no question that it also poses dangers. Sexual predators have used Internet chat rooms to arrange meetings with teenagers and young children, for example. Also, pornography is readily

Frequency of Computer Use

"Do you ever use a computer or word processor at home?"

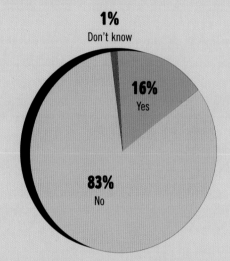

1%
Don't know

16%
Yes

1987

83%
No

Polls taken June 1987; 1,219 total respondents
Source: The Gallup Organization

"Do you ever use a computer or word processor at the place where you work?"

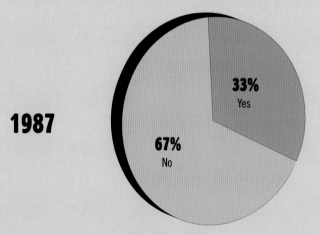

33%
Yes

1987

67%
No

Polls taken June 1987; 1,219 total respondents
Source: The Gallup Organization

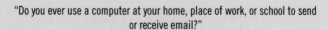

"Do you ever use a computer at your home, place of work, or school to send or receive email?"

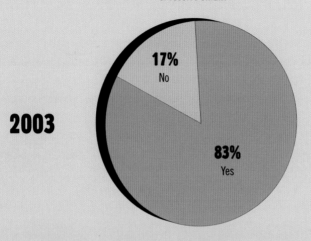

2003

17%
No

83%
Yes

Polls taken April 2003; 795 total respondents
Source: The Gallup Organization

Daily Internet Use, by Age, 2002–2003

"How much time, if at all, do you personally spend using the Internet?"

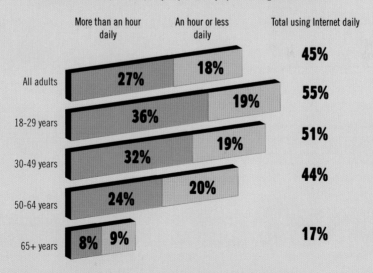

	More than an hour daily	An hour or less daily	Total using Internet daily
All adults	27%	18%	45%
18-29 years	36%	19%	55%
30-49 years	32%	19%	51%
50-64 years	24%	20%	44%
65+ years	8%	9%	17%

Polls taken December 2002–December 2003; 2,012 total respondents
Source: The Gallup Organization

available over the Internet, as is gambling. Computer viruses are spread through e-mail and can wreak havoc. Privacy has also become an issue. In 2000, a Gallup poll found that 53 percent of Americans are "very concerned," while 29 percent said they are "somewhat concerned," that the Internet could be used to violate their right to privacy.

And then there is spam—the junk e-mail generated electronically that sends unwanted advertising messages into millions of e-mail accounts every day. A 2003 Gallup poll found that 67 percent of respondents regard spam as a problem, and that 37 percent of Americans either quit their e-mail companies or

E-mail and instant messaging programs have changed the ways in which many Americans communicate.

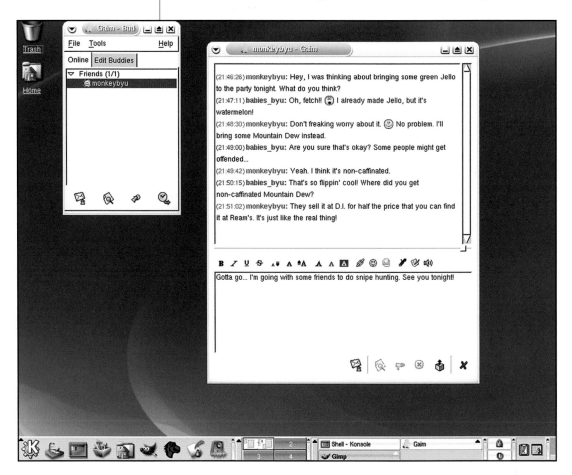

considered quitting because they thought the companies let in too much spam. A Gallup analysis com-
mented, "That's a pretty substantial percentage when
one considers that the burden of coordinating and
communicating the change makes switching e-mail
accounts as much of a headache as changing banks."

Most e-mail companies have already implemented
filters to block spam, although, certainly, much of it slips
through. Still, the technology that has enabled computers to radically impact people's lives continues to
change in the 21st century. The machine that previously
occupied a whole floor in a university building and
dimmed the lights of a major city can now be carried in
a pocket and run off a battery — and it can perform tasks
that Herman Hollerith, Howard Aiken, and perhaps
even Steve Wozniak never dreamed possible.

8 LOOKING TO THE FUTURE

A NASA artist drew this speculative idea of what a future mission to Mars might look like. In recent years, NASA's robotic rovers have explored areas of the "red planet," and in 2004 President George W. Bush proposed a new space program with the goal of one day landing a manned mission on Mars.

One wonders what Charles Duell would have said if he had headed the U.S. Patents Office in 1999 instead of in 1899. Looking over the state of American technology at the end of the 20th century, he would have seen supercomputers, spaceships, and stem cell research. At the same time, he would have realized there was even more on the horizon.

Predicting the technology that will be familiar in American life a century from now is an art best left to science fiction writers. Without question, in the past, such writers have made accurate predictions. For instance, the 19th-century French writer Jules Verne accurately predicted the course of future space travel in his 1865 book *From the Earth to the Moon*. In his 1870 book *20,000 Leagues Under the Sea*, Verne predicted that a submarine would be able to travel the oceans quickly and silently, armed with the deadliest weapons known to man. Similarly, writing in her 1818 novel *Frankenstein*, Mary Wollstonecraft Shelley predicted that electricity would be necessary to animate life in the laboratory—just as Ian Wilmut discovered when he cloned Dolly the sheep nearly two centuries later.

Still, for anybody anxious to take a peek at the future, there are some developments occurring today that could lead to tremendous advancements during the next few years. For example, the United States is involved in an international effort to develop a nuclear fusion project. Fusion reactions provide the energy that powers the stars in the sky, including the sun. In a fusion reaction, the intense heat of millions of degrees fuses atoms together, making them spit out energy in the form of neutrons. Fusion reactions are clean and, unlike fission reactions, do not leave behind spent fuel that is hazardous to people and the environment. Yet the price tag for fusion experimenting is high—the effort known as the International Thermonuclear Experimental Reactor is estimated to cost $5 billion. Nevertheless, if fusion reactors become a reality, they could go a long way toward solving energy needs in the United States and elsewhere.

Another area that may lead to new technologies is the space program. Since the Apollo program ended during the 1970s, manned spaceflights have been limited to orbiting the Earth. Although NASA has sent unmanned probes to distant planets and beyond, plans to revive manned flights out of Earth orbit have often lacked political, public, and financial support in the United States. Without the competition of a race for space with the Soviet Union, Americans have had little interest in manned missions to the planets.

In 1991, a Gallup poll asked Americans whether they would favor a manned mission to Mars. Just 8 percent of the respondents found a manned mission "very important," while 28 percent found such a venture "somewhat important."

In 2004, President George W. Bush proposed a revival of manned exploration of space, suggesting that NASA pursue establishing a base on the moon as a first step in a program to one day land astronauts on Mars. "Mankind is drawn to the heavens for the same reason we were once drawn to unknown lands and across the open sea," Bush said. "We choose to explore space because doing so improves our lives and lifts our national spirit."

Bush proposed the new manned missions 35 years after the first moon landing. A Gallup poll in early 2004 showed Americans still believing that the space program represented the epitome of the nation's technological abilities. Shortly before Bush's speech,

NASA landed two spacecraft on Mars, each dispatching robotic rovers that conducted observations and scientific analyses. Seventy-two percent of respondents to a 2004 Gallup poll thought the Mars robotic landing missions represented major achievements. A separate Gallup poll taken in 2004 found 68 percent of Americans in agreement with the statement "the quality of our daily lives has benefited from the knowledge and technology that have come from our nation's space program."

In a Gallup analysis of the poll, Jim Banke, a spokesman for the Space Foundation, an organization that promotes space science, said, "Just look at the Weather Channel. Those accurate forecasts come from satellites, and satellites are in space. Or just go into any electronics store. I'd bet that 80% of the products there are available because of the space program . . . increased data storage, satellite television and radio, global positioning systems, the list goes on and on."

As for manned missions to Mars, Americans were not yet ready to endorse Bush's plan, mostly because of the multi-billion-dollar cost involved. Just 26 percent of respondents to a Gallup poll said NASA's funding should be increased to pay for programs such as a manned mission to Mars.

Still, history teaches us that if Congress decides not to fund a manned Mars mission, then in time somebody else may figure out a way to fly space travelers to the distant planets. It may not occur in the 21st century or perhaps even in the 22nd century, but there is no question that science and technology have always found ways to conquer the unknown, as long as somebody has been willing to wonder, "What if?"

abacus—an ancient calculating device, consisting of a simple frame holding wires threaded through beads, which can be slid up and down to perform mathematical computations.

electromagnetism—magnetism developed by a current of electricity, usually by coiling a wire carrying current around a soft metal object.

embryo—earliest stage in the development of the fetus.

euthanize—to cause painless death in order to relieve suffering.

fallout—term describing the descent of radioactive particles through the atmosphere after a nuclear explosion.

fission—the splitting of the atomic nucleus, resulting in the release of large amounts of energy.

frequencies—in radio, the variations of waves carrying the signal.

fusion—the union of atomic nuclei to form heavier nuclei, which can result in the release of large amounts of energy.

Great Depression—period of American history, from 1929 to the late 1930s, marked by economic collapse, high unemployment, and widespread poverty.

medium—a channel or system of communication, information, or entertainment.

physicist—scientist who pursues knowledge of the natural laws that govern motion, matter, and energy.

piston—a sliding piece that fits inside a cylinder, connected to a rod that it pushes when it reacts to a controlled explosion; the rod provides the motion that drives the engine.

radioactivity—emission of waves or particles from certain elements used as fuel in, for example, nuclear power plants or nuclear weapons.

schematic—a diagram, usually employing universally known symbols, of an electrical circuit, mechanical device, or building plan, for example.

Andrews, Paul. *How the Web Was Won: Microsoft from Windows to the Web*. New York: Broadway Books, 1999.

Bijlefeld, Marjolijn, and Robert Burke. *It Came from Outer Space: Everyday Products and Ideas from the Space Program*. Westport, CT: Greenwood Press, 2003.

Garwin, Richard L., and Georges Charpak. *Megawatts and Megatons: The Future of Nuclear Power and Nuclear Weapons*. Chicago: University of Chicago Press, 2001.

Lindsey, James M., and Michael O'Hanlon. *Defending America: The Case for Limited National Missile Defense*. Washington, D.C.: Brookings Institution Press, 2001.

Manes, Stephen, and Paul Andrews. *Gates: How Microsoft's Mogul Reinvented an Industry—And Made Himself the Richest Man in America*. New York: Doubleday, 1993.

McGee, Glenn, editor. *The Human Cloning Debate*. Albany, Calif.: Berkeley Hills Books, 2002.

Moschovitis, Christos, Hilary Poole, Tami Schuyler, and Theresa M. Senft. *History of the Internet: A Chronology, 1843 to the Present*. Santa Barbara, Calif.: ABC-Clio, 1999.

Mould, Richard F. *Chernobyl Record: The Definitive History of the Chernobyl Catastrophe*. New York: Institute of Physics Publishing, 2000.

Powaski, Ronald E. *March to Armageddon: The United States and the Nuclear Arms Race, 1939 to the Present*. New York: Oxford University Press, 1987.

———. *Return to Armageddon: The United States and the Nuclear Arms Race, 1981–1999*. New York: Oxford University Press, 2003.

Sagan, Carl. *Cosmos*. New York: Random House, 1980.

Spangenburg, Ray, and Diane K. Moser. *The History of Science from 1895 to 1945*. New York: Facts on File, 1994.

Wolfe, Tom, *The Right Stuff*. New York: Farrar, Straus and Giroux, 1979.

DISCOVERY OF THE DOUBLE HELIX

http://usatoday.com/news/science/2003-02-24-dna-cover_x.htm

USA Today's series of stories marking the fiftieth anniversary of the discovery of the double helix can be accessed at this site.

THE GALLUP ORGANIZATION

www.gallup.com

The website of the national polling institute includes polling data and analyses on hundreds of topics.

HERMAN HOLLERITH

www.columbia.edu/acis/history/hollerith.html

A biography of computer pioneer Herman Hollerith is maintained by Columbia University, the school where Hollerith earned his undergraduate and graduate degrees. The website includes descriptions of Hollerith's inventions, including the Hollerith Electric Tabulating System.

LINDBERGH

www.pbs.org/wgbh/amex/lindbergh/

The companion website to the PBS television documentary *Lindbergh* serves as a resource on the life of Charles Lindbergh and the flight of the *Spirit of St. Louis.*

OLD TIME RADIO: A SOUNDBITE HISTORY

www.otr.com/hindenburg.html

Students can hear radio commentator Herb Morrison's dramatic description of the *Hindenburg* disaster by accessing this website.

RACE FOR THE SUPERBOMB

www.pbs.org/wgbh/amex/bomb/index.html

Companion website to the PBS television documentary *Race for the Superbomb*, which chronicled the program to develop atomic weapons in the 1950s and 1960s.

SPUTNIK AND THE DAWN OF THE SPACE AGE

www.hq.nasa.gov/office/pao/History/sputnik/index.html

NASA has established this Internet resource to chronicle the history of the Sputnik satellite launches; students can hear a digitized recording of the beeps the satellite transmitted as it passed overhead.

THIRTIETH ANNIVERSARY OF APOLLO 11: 1969–1999

http://nssdc.gsfc.nasa.gov/planetary/lunar/apollo_11_30th.html

A comprehensive history of the Apollo 11 flight and moon landing, compiled by the National Aeronautics and Space Administration. This Internet page celebrating the thirtieth anniversary of the flight features many photographs and digitized recordings of the astronauts' transmissions from the moon.

BOOKS AND PERIODICALS

Belair, Felix Jr. "Nautilus Sails Under the Pole and 1,830 Miles of Arctic Icecap in Pacific-to-Atlantic Passage," *New York Times*, August 9, 1958.

Brooks, John. *Telephone: The First Hundred Years*. New York: Harper & Row, 1976.

Carlson, Darren K. "Space: To Infinity and Beyond on a Budget," Gallup Poll, August 17, 2004.

Clinton, Bill. "Remarks Announcing the Prohibition on Federal Funding for Cloning Human Beings," *Weekly Compilation of Presidential Documents*, March 10, 1997.

Dickson, Paul. *Sputnik: The Shock of the Century*. New York: Walker and Co., 2001.

Fitzgerald, Frances. *Way Out There in the Blue: Reagan, Star Wars and the End of the Cold War*. New York: Simon & Schuster, 2000.

Flowers, Charles. *A Science Odyssey: 100 Years of Discovery*. New York: William Morrow and Co., 1998.

Gallup, George. "Most See Need for Nuclear Power, But Many Concerned About Safety," Gallup Poll, July 22, 1976.

———. "Nearly 12 Million Families Taking Nuclear War Measures," Public Opinion News Service, August 20, 1961.

———. "One Year After Sputnik: Public Passes Judgment on Who's Ahead—U.S. or Russia?" Public Opinion News Service, October 3, 1958.

———. "Public Not Greatly Concerned About Chances of Nuclear War," Public Opinion News Service, July 14, 1961.

———. "Public Rejects Idea of 'Winnable Nuclear War,'" Gallup Poll, August 2, 1981.

Gallup Jr., George. "Chernobyl Revives Public's Qualms About Nuclear Power Generation," Gallup Poll, July 24, 1986.

———. "'Star Wars' Support Grows, But Many Like Gorbachev's Counterproposal," Gallup Poll, November 17, 1985.

Gibbs, Nancy. "Human Cloning: Baby, It's You! And You, and You," *Time*, February 19, 2001.

Goldstein, Norm. *The History of Television*. New York: Portland House, 1991.

Halberstam, David. *The Reckoning*. New York: William Morrow and Co., 1986.

Heppenheimer, T.A. *First Flight: The Wright Brothers and the Invention of the Airplane*. Hoboken, N.J.: John Wiley & Sons, 2003.

Hurt, Harry III. *For All Mankind*. New York: Atlantic Monthly Press, 1988.

Jones, Jeffrey M. "Almost All E-Mail Users Say Internet, E-Mail Have Made Lives Better," Gallup Poll, July 23, 2001.

Kluger, Jeffrey. "Will We Follow the Sheep?" *Time*, March 10, 1997.

Linzmayer, Owen L. *Apple Confidential 2.0: The Definitive History of the World's Most Colorful Company*. San Francisco: No Starch Press, 2004.

Lyons, Lynda. "Internet Use: What's Age Got to Do With It?" Gallup Poll, March 16, 2004.

Newport, Frank, and Joseph Carroll. "American E-mailers Increasingly Fed Up With Computer Spam," Gallup Poll, May 20, 2003.

Parrish, Thomas. *The Submarine: A History*. New York: Viking, 2004.

Saad, Lydia. "Few Web Users Paying Close Attention to Internet Privacy Issue," Gallup Poll, Nov. 27, 2000.

———. "Cloning Humans Is a Turn Off to Most Americans," Gallup Poll, May 16, 2002.

Stashower, Daniel. *The Boy Genius and the Mogul: The Untold Story of Television*. New York: Broadway Books, 2002.

"U.S. Seen Leading in Missile Race in Poll Since Space Shots," Public Opinion News Service, June 7, 1961.

Walker, J. Samuel. *Three Mile Island: A Nuclear Crisis in Historical Perspective*. Berkeley, Calif.: University of California Press, 2004.

White, Theodore. *The Making of the President 1960*. New York: Atheneum Publishers, 1961.

Wise, David, and Thomas B. Ross. *The Invisible Government*. New York: Vintage, 1974.

INTERNET REPORTS

Bellis, Mary. "Inventors of the Modern Computer," http://inventors.about.com/library/weekly/aa121598.htm.

"Brave New World," CBS News, February 12, 2001, www.cbsnews.com/stories/2001/02/11/tech/main271100.shtml

Friend, Tim. "Elusive Gene Therapy Forges On," *USA Today*, February 23, 2003, www.usatoday.com/news/health/2003-02-23-gene-therapy_x.htm

"Gene Therapy," PBS Online Newshour, www.ps.org/newshour/bb/health/jan-june00/gene_therapy_2-2.html

Launius, Roger D. "Sputnik and the Origins of the Space Age," National Aeronautics and Space Administration, www.hq.nasa.gov/office/pao/History/sputnik/sputorig.html

"The Manhattan Project," http://library.thinkquest.org/17940/texts/timeline/manhattan.html

Postman, Neil. "Philo Farnsworth," *Time*, March 29, 1999, www.time.com/time/time100/scientist/profile/farnsworth.html

"A Short History of the Double Helix as We Know It," *USA Today*, February 21, 2003, www.usatoday.com/news/science/2003-02-21-dna-cover-timeline_x.htm

Spring, Kathleen McGinn. "The Story of Color Television," U.S. 1, November 14, 2001, www.princetoninfo.com/200111/11114c01.html

Twist, Jo. "Rutan Ready to Realize Vision," BBC News Online, September 25, 2004, www.bbc.co.uk/1/hi/sci/tech/3676312.stm

U.S. Naval Air Engineering Station at Lakehurst, www.lakehurst.navy.mil/nlweb/hindenb.html

COMPUTER HISTORY MUSEUM

1401 North Shoreline Boulevard
Mountain View, California 94043
650-810-1010
Website: www.computerhistory.org

More than 5,500 artifacts that trace the history of computers from
their earliest days are on display at the museum; visitors to the
museum's Web site can access documents that date back to when
the abacus was the most user-friendly computer.

JOHN F. KENNEDY LIBRARY AND MUSEUM

Columbia Point
Boston, Massachusetts 02125
617-514-1600
866-JFK-1960
Website: www.jfklibrary.org

Visitors to the museum can watch tapes of President Kennedy's televised debates with Vice President Richard M. Nixon; exhibits are also
devoted to the Cuban missile crisis, the birth of the U.S. space program, and other important events that occurred during Kennedy's
presidency.

MUSEUM OF BROADCAST COMMUNICATIONS

400 North State Street
Chicago, Illinois 60610
312-245-8200
Website: www.museum.tv

The museum has archived more than eighty-five thousand tapes of
radio and television programming as well as many artifacts from the
early days of broadcasting, including the camera used to televise the
first Nixon-Kennedy debate and thousands of pages of documents,
such as song sheets and scripts from early radio programs.

NATIONAL AERONAUTICS AND SPACE ADMINISTRATION HEADQUARTERS LIBRARY

300 E St., SW, suite 1J20
Washington, DC 20546
202-358-0168
Website: www.hq.nasa.gov/office/hqlibrary

The space agency maintains an extensive library of books, documents, and magazine and newspaper articles about the history of the nation's space program.

NATIONAL AUTOMOBILE MUSEUM

10 South Lake Street
Reno, NV 89501-1558
775-333-9300
Website: www.automuseum.org

The museum displays more than two hundred vintage cars, including six Model T Fords as well as other vehicles that date back to 1892.

NATIONAL MUSEUM OF NUCLEAR SCIENCE AND HISTORY

1905 Mountain Road NW
Albuquerque, New Mexico 87104
505-245-2137
Website: www.atomicmuseum.com

Formerly the National Atomic Museum, the facility traces the history of the atomic age in the United States, starting in the 1940s when New Mexico was the site of the earliest research and testing involving nuclear weapons.

SMITHSONIAN INSTITUTION NATIONAL AIR AND SPACE MUSEUM

National Mall
Sixth Street and Independence Avenue SW
Washington, DC 20560
202-633-1000
Website: www.nasm.si.edu

The history of aviation and spaceflight is chronicled at the world-famous museum in Washington DC, where visitors can see the Wright brothers' *Flyer*, Chuck Yeager's X-1, Charles Lindbergh's *Spirit of St. Louis*, and several other famous planes and spacecraft on display.

U.S. NUCLEAR REGULATORY COMMISSION
Office of Public Affairs
Washington, DC 20555
301-415-8200
800-368-5642
Website: www.nrc.gov

The federal agency regulates nuclear power plants in the United States; visitors to the agency's Web site can find information on security and safety issues concerning nuclear power, storage and disposal of spent nuclear fuel and waste, and licensure of current and proposed plants.

WRIGHT BROTHERS NATIONAL MEMORIAL
1401 National Park Drive
Manteo, NC 27954
252-441 7430
Website: www.nps.gov/wrbr/pphtml/contact.html

The National Park Service maintains a memorial to Wilbur and Orville Wright at the scene of the historic first powered flight on Kill Devil Hill near Kitty Hawk, North Carolina; the memorial includes a sixty-foot granite monument perched atop the hill.

Numbers in ***bold italic*** refer to captions and graphs.

INDEX

Page:
3:          National Aeronautics and Space Administration
8:          Library of Congress; (left) PhotoDisc; (center) PhotoDisc;
            (right) Digital Vision
11:         Erich Lessing/Art Resource, NY
12:         National Aeronautics and Space Administration
14:         Library of Congress
18:         Library of Congress
20:         © OTTN Publishing
21:         Library of Congress
22:         Library of Congress
25:         (top) Library of Congress; (bottom) Library of Congress
26:         Library of Congress
27:         (top) Library of Congress; (bottom) Library of Congress
28:         Library of Congress
30–31:   Courtesy of Public Broadcasting Service/PBS.org
32:         © OTTN Publishing
35:         Photo No. KN-C20515 in the John F. Kennedy Library, Boston
36:         © OTTN Publishing
39:         Bettmann/Corbis
42:         © OTTN Publishing
44:         Private Collection
46:         National Aeronautics and Space Administration
51:         © OTTN Publishing
52:         National Aeronautics and Space Administration
54:         (both) National Aeronautics and Space Administration
57:         National Aeronautics and Space Administration
59:         © OTTN Publishing
60:         National Aeronautics and Space Administration
62:         National Archives
65:         Library of Congress
66:         © OTTN Publishing
68:         Library of Congress
69:         Universal Pictures/Courtesy of Getty Images
71:         © OTTN Publishing
72:         National Aeronautics and Space Administration
77:         Time Life Pictures/NASA/Time Life Pictures/Getty Images
78:         Jim Mamay (jbmamay@ahnwu.com) AHNWU.COM
81:         (both) Daniel Mordzinski/AFP/Getty Images
83:         © OTTN Publishing
85:         Stephen Ferry/Liaison/Getty Images
89:         Tim Sloan/AFP/Getty Images
90:         © OTTN Publishing
92:         Hulton Archive/Getty Images
98:         Library of Congress
101:        Ted Thai/Time Life Pictures/Getty Images
104:        © OTTN Publishing
106:        © OTTN Publishing
108–109:   NASA/Pat Rawlings, SAIC

CONTRIBUTORS

For almost three-quarters of a century, the **GALLUP POLL** has measured the attitudes and opinions of the American public about the major events and the most important political, social, and economic issues of the day. Founded in 1935 by Dr. George Gallup, the Gallup Poll was the world's first public opinion poll based on scientific sampling procedures. For most of its history, the Gallup Poll was sponsored by the nation's largest newspapers, which published two to four of Gallup's public opinion reports each week. Poll findings, which covered virtually every major news event and important issue facing the nation and the world, were reported in a variety of media. More recently, the poll has been conducted in partnership with CNN and USA Today. All of Gallup's findings, including many opinion trends dating back to the 1930s and 1940s, are accessible at www.gallup.com.

ALEC M. GALLUP is chairman of The Gallup Poll in the United States, and Chairman of The Gallup Organization Ltd. in Great Britain. He also serves as a director of The Gallup Organisation, Europe; Gallup China; and Gallup Hungary. He has been employed by Gallup since 1959 and has directed or played key roles in many of the company's most ambitious and innovative projects, including Gallup's 2002 "Survey of Nine Islamic Nations"; the "Global Cities Project"; the "Global Survey on Attitudes Towards AIDS"; the 25-nation "Health of The Planet Survey"; and the ongoing "Survey of Consumer Attitudes and Lifestyles in China." Mr. Gallup also oversees several annual "social audits," including "Black and White Relations in the United States," an investigation of attitudes and perceptions concerning the state of race relations, and "Survey of the Public's Attitudes Toward the Public Schools," which tracks attitudes on educational issues.

Mr. Gallup's educational background includes undergraduate work at Princeton University and the University of Iowa. He undertook graduate work in communications and journalism at Stanford University, and studied marketing and advertising research at New York University. His publications include *The Great American Success Story* (with George Gallup, Jr.; Dow Jones-Irwin, 1986), *Presidential Approval: A Source Book* (with George Edwards; Johns Hopkins University Press, 1990), *The Gallup Poll Cumulative Index: Public Opinion* 1935–1997 (Scholarly Resources, 1999), and *British Political Opinion 1937–2000: The Gallup Polls* (with Anthony King and Robert Wybrow; Politicos Publishing, 2001).

HAL MARCOVITZ has written more than 70 books for young readers. His other titles in the GALLUP MAJOR TRENDS AND EVENTS series include *Abortion, Race Relations, Drug and Alcohol Abuse,* and *Health Care.* He lives in Chalfont, Pennsylvania, with his wife Gail and daughters Ashley and Michelle, and enjoys writing fiction. He is the author of the satirical novel *Painting the White House.*